Information Nation

Praise for *Information Nation*

Kahn and Blair have managed to craft into one superb, readable book the information both the novice and specialist need to create an effective Information Management Compliance program. *Information Nation* is one of the best resources on compliance, in any risk topic, that I have ever read.

> *Win Swenson, Former Deputy General Counsel and Chair of the Organizational Guidelines Working Group, U.S. Sentencing Commission; Partner, Compliance Systems Legal Group*

Managing information to support compliance is a monumental challenge for business and IT professionals today. This book provides straightforward guidelines to help them meet this challenge.

> *David B. Wright, President, LEGATO Software*

A practical roadmap for implementing a successful compliance program. It completes the picture on information use in commercial enterprises by laying the foundation for good corporate governance, now a key strategic initiative for competing in today's global business environment.

> *Andy Lawrence, Eastman Kodak Company, One of Business Ethics "100 Best Corporate Citizens for 2003"*

Many companies overlook the importance of data management. *Information Nation* is a wake-up call that reminds us all that improperly managed information is a huge liability. The book is a great starting point for those that are just beginning to put a policy in place, and for those experienced individuals who are interested in performing a reality check on their existing Information Management Compliance methodology.

> *Paul Butticaz, Vice President, SunTrust Robinson Humphrey*

At a time when there is a pressing need to improve the way information is managed, Kahn and Blair's message and methodology are right on. This book is much more than a "must read." It is a "must do" action plan for achieving compliance and mitigating risks in today's new world.

Robert F. Williams, Cohasset Associates, Inc.

Information Nation provides practical advice, based on real-world examples, for anyone faced with the formidable task of developing and maintaining an effective Information Management program. An easy to read volume, packed with useful information designed to assist the legal professional or corporate manager in implementing efficient and legally sound policies and procedures.

Candace S. Erisen, Counsel, Cinergy Services, Inc.

One stop shopping for everything you need to know about Information Management Compliance. *Information Nation* covers the gamut of legal issues and the business risks with comprehensive analysis and advice in plain English. For an issue of increasing importance to businesses, you won't find a better work under one cover.

Marc Martin, Of Counsel, Kirkpatrick & Lockhart, LLP

IMC is rapidly evolving into a paramount issue for organizations to address NOW. *Information Nation* is an excellent resource for technology management executives and professionals in understanding the inherent vulnerabilities of existing information management practices and implementing appropriate safeguards for the future.

Evan Wagner, Network Design and Security consultant

Other Books from Randolph Kahn

E-Mail Rules: A Business Guide To Managing Policies, Security, and Legal Issues for E-Mail and Digital Communication

INFORMATION NATION

POLICIES AND PROCEDURES

EXECUTIVE RESPONSIBILITY

DELEGATION

COMMUNICATION AND TRAINING

AUDITING AND MONITORING

EFFECTIVE AND CONSISTENT ENFORCEMENT

CONTINUOUS IMPROVEMENT

Seven Keys
to Information
Management
Compliance

aiim

Silver Spring, Maryland, United States
Worcester, United Kingdom

**Randolph A. Kahn, ESQ. and
Barclay T. Blair**

This publication is designed to provide accurate and authoritative information in regard to the subject matter covered. It is sold with the understanding that neither the publisher nor the authors, through this book, are engaged in rendering legal, accounting, or other professional service. If legal advice or other expert assistance is required, the services of a competent professional person should be sought.

Library of Congress Cataloging-in-Publication Data

Kahn, Randolph.

Information Nation: Seven Keys to Information Management Compliance/Randolph A. Kahn, ESQ., and Barclay T. Blair.

p. cm.

Includes bibliographical references and index.

ISBN 0-89258-402-5 (pbk.)

1. Management information systems-United States. 2. Information technology-United States-Management. 3. Business records-Data processing-Management. 4. Business records-Law and legislation-United States. 5. Disclosure of information-Law and legislation-United States. I. Blair, Barclay T. II. Title.

HD30.213.K34 2004
658.4'038—dc22
2004000366

ISBN 0-89258-402-5

Cover illustration by Rings Leighton Design Group.

Special discounts on bulk quantities of AIIM publications are available upon request. For details, contact AIIM Publications, 1100 Wayne Avenue, Suite 1100, Silver Spring, MD, 20910, U.S. www.aiim.org

Randolph A. Kahn, ESQ.

In loving memory of my mother
Lillian Kahn.

To my family,
Melissa, Dylan, Lily, and Teddy
who make life such a joy.

Special thanks to the
Kahn Consulting team and
our clients, partners, and friends.

Barclay T. Blair

To Margie.
To Brian.
To Randy.
To Farnese.

Contents

Contents

Forward

by Jay Cohen, ESQ.

Time and time again, Information Management Compliance failures have proven to be devastating. Companies flounder, and some go away altogether. Customer confidence is shaken and business is lost. Laws are broken, data is not protected, and systems are overburdened. Organizational mismanagement of information is far too common-place today and we are now reeling—trying to figure out what to do next.

The time has never been better for a book like *Information Nation: Seven Keys to Information Management Compliance*. It is a unique and practical guide for IT professionals, business executives, lawyers, records managers, and compliance officers on how best to manage information according to a disciplined methodology that will minimize organizational risks and failures.

These are not sentiments that can be applied to many books. But, *Information Nation* is no ordinary book. It provides the clearest, best organized, and most useful means of addressing the considerable challenges posed by a whole host of information management issues. Issues that we now know can threaten an organization's very existence, especially if the warnings and lessons in this book are not understood and heeded.

No matter your position at your organization, or the current stage of your Information Management efforts, this book will provide you with practical steps for better protecting your organization's business and legal interests. If you don't have an Information or Records Management program today, this book will help you create and implement a comprehensive approach that will work for your organization, day in and day out. If you already have an Information Management program, this book will enable you to measure your program's effectiveness and mitigate risks.

Organizations with inadequate Information Management programs are equally in need of Kahn and Blair's extraordinary skills, expertise, and advice as are those that have no program at all. I for one learned the hard way that failing to have a compliant Information Management program can be devastating.

Let me draw on that personal experience to illustrate the point.

I first met Randy in 1997, when I was a compliance officer at a previous firm—a large, multi-national institution. Our organization—perhaps like yours—had a records retention program, complete with policies and procedures, retention schedules, a thick binder, and even a warehouse or two where we stored boxes of paper files. Like most companies these days, we were defendants in a lawsuit and, in connection with that lawsuit, we were asked by the court to "retain all records and other information" that might be relevant to the controversy (such a request is routinely made in just about every lawsuit). Our company sent out notices to all employees, in accordance with the Records Management policy, reminding them to comply with that "preservation order." The job was done, and we could rest assured that the organization was protected.

Not exactly.

That is where my company stood when I got a call at home on a Sunday in December, to report to headquarters. It turned out that a few employees had destroyed paper and electronic records that were "relevant" to the lawsuit—and it hardly mattered to the court that this destruction may have been innocent or negligent, rather than intentional. The point was that the information was gone, and the court wanted to know what the most senior executives of the company had done to prevent the destruction. The court asked a series of questions—both about our program in general and about its application in this case—indicating its view that our responsibilities went well beyond just having a policy and issuing a notice.

We were forced to ask ourselves many painful questions:

- Who was responsible for the Records Management program in our organization?

- How and when had we communicated with our employees about the program?

- What had we done to train employees about the program, and what would happen if they failed to comply?

- What had we done BEFORE the preservation order was issued to assure that relevant records were around to be retained?

- Did the program incorporate electronic records, as well as paper files?

- How did the company ensure that employees were complying with the policies and program requirements?

- Had there been any audits, compliance reviews, or similar efforts?

- What did the company do to ensure that the preservation notice in this matter was received, understood, and complied with by each and every employee throughout the organization?

- What, if any, follow-up communication was undertaken?

- Could we identify and locate ALL of the relevant information that was needed?

- Did we have, and implement, a process to quickly investigate and respond to instances of non-compliance?

- How did we document compliance with the program in general, and with the specific retention request at issue?

We could not, unfortunately, provide satisfactory answers to ALL of these questions. As a result, the court converted the destruction of documents by just a couple of individuals into an ORGANIZATIONAL failure and responsibility. The resulting institutional damages—in fines, administrative and litigation expenses, and loss of reputation—far exceeded the value of the lost documents. That is what you want to avoid, and to do that you need to start now.

This book is by far the best resource that I know of to help you take on the complex challenge of managing your information assets. It is the only resource I have seen that is organized around the kinds of questions that courts, regulators, and prosecutors are going to ask, and that provides the answers they expect. The methodology advanced by *Information Nation* is a compliance framework that can be applied to all Information Management activities, and will tell the courts, regulators, stockholders, executives, boards, and the public that you take your Information Management responsibilities seriously.

And if you already have a problem with Information Management, *Information Nation* and the authors can help you resolve it. Mr. Kahn came to our rescue during a critical time in our company's history. With his help—and in far less time than anyone thought possible—we built and implemented a nationwide Information Management Compliance program (not just a record retention policy) that the court accepted and that our company could be proud of.

I have had occasion to work with Randy, Barclay, and the rest of the Kahn Consulting team on a number of projects since this experience. They represent the rarest combination of technical knowledge, business acuity, legal skill, and practical experience, and that wisdom and experience come through on every page of this important work.

In my own experience as a compliance executive, I have come to view organizational compliance efforts as trying to accomplish two things: first, to make it as least likely as possible that individuals in the organization will violate their legal and compliance responsibilities; and second, to ensure that if someone does violate that trust, it is viewed as an individual and not an organizational problem, because of everything that the organization has done to address the first goal. This book gives you the tools to accomplish both goals when it comes to Information Management Compliance.

Jay Cohen, ESQ.
Chief Compliance Officer
The Mony Group

Preface

by John F. Mancini

Welcome to the world of Information Management Compliance!

AIIM International conducts frequent surveys to analyze trends within the Enterprise Content Management (ECM) industry and to identify issues and best practices related to the application of ECM technologies. Recent surveys have revealed several themes that highlight the critical need for *Information Nation: Seven Keys to Information Management Compliance:*

- The fundamentals of business documentation—the processes by which organizations prove what, when, who, why, and how they conduct their operations—have been turned on their head in the past five years.

- Electronic information has become the dominant means to document business processes.

- The amount and complexity of electronic information that must be kept to document business processes is increasing exponentially *by the day*. So too is the sophistication of those who challenge organizations based on the vulnerability of their electronic information.

- Most organizations have not recognized the scope of the change that has occurred, and are thus facing cascading risk and liability within their organizations.

In fall 2003, AIIM and Kahn Consulting surveyed over 1,000 individuals on their email management capabilities. What we found is that most organizations clearly rely on email to do business. For example, 84% use email to discuss operating and product strategies. Seventy-one percent use email to negotiate contracts. Sixty-four percent use email to convey confidential information. However, despite using email for such sensitive and valuable business activities, few organizations apply even the most basic disciplines associated with prudent records management to their email system. When asked, "Do you have a policy that outlines where, how, and by whom email is retained?" only 36% reported this basic level of competency. And email is only a part of the problem. The same patterns and vulnerability exist for all forms of electronic information. The volume of this information is staggering—there is currently more information on the hard drive of a typical computer than can be read in a single lifetime—and current controls are marginal.

What is to be done about this? I think this book provides important lessons to help organizations address the Information Management Compliance problem. I believe the key is to recognize that the solution lies in striking the right balance between two often-conflicting demands—the demand for greater operational efficiency and the demand for improved compliance and standardization.

The technology of information management increasingly enables organizations to do things better, faster, and cheaper. At the same time, 90% of the information that organizations must manage is unstructured—information that does not neatly fall into the rows and columns of a traditional database. Moreover, unstructured information is at the heart of business processes. And processes cannot be standardized and improved until this flow of information is standardized, digitized, and managed. So, within organizations there is a constant push to rapidly deploy technologies to reduce costs and improve processes. This is a world populated by the IT departments and line-of-business managers within organizations.

At the same time, governments and courts at all levels—local, state, federal—are making increasing demands for the trustworthiness, accuracy, and reliability of electronic information. There is a temptation to think of this as just a "Sarbanes-Oxley problem" or a "HIPAA problem." But I believe this is part of a long-term trend toward defining what transparency and accountability of organizations means in an electronic era. This is creating a need to reduce the risks associated with management of electronic information. This is creating a need to more clearly define and measure the processes associated with management of this information—a roundabout way of saying a need for greater "compliance." This is a world often defined by the legal, risk management, and compliance departments of organizations.

This book pulls together these often-conflicting worlds of information management and compliance and defines a framework for looking at them *together*. The only way organizations can handle these conflicting demands is by looking at them through the prism of *Information Management Compliance*. It is no longer enough to simply automate a single department's processes, independent of the broader information management structure within organizations. It is no longer enough to assume that "someone" down in the organization will be responsible for the management of electronic information critical to documenting the business; the courts will hold the CEO accountable in the end. It is no longer enough to implement technology without a framework of policies and procedures—and a means to educate employees on those policies and procedures and to hold them accountable.

These issues will not be solved overnight. This book takes enormous strides toward defining the seven key steps to get organizations started down the path of 21st century accountability and responsibility. AIIM is proud to be a part of bringing this critical message to the public.

John F. Mancini
President
AIIM

Author's Acknowledgements

Many of our friends and colleagues contributed to this book by volunteering their valuable time to review and comment on the manuscript. For this we wish to extend our thanks to:

Andy Lawrence, Ben Wilson, Candace Erisen, David B. Wright, Evan Wagner, Jay Cohen, Jeanne Caldwell, Marc Martin, Michael Power, Paul Butticaz, Robert F. Williams, and Win Swenson.

Also, thanks to James Hospodarsky for his valuable contribution on Change Management. Special thanks to David M. Freedman for his editorial contribution.

Introduction:

Welcome to a New Era of Information Management

> *It might be useful to consider reminding the [Enron] engagement team of our documentation and retention policy. It will be helpful to make sure that we have complied with the policy. Let me know if you have any questions.*[1]

Email from Nancy Temple, Arthur Andersen in-house attorney,
October 12, 2001

Under normal circumstances, an email message like this might be considered innocuous, or even commendable. All companies should regularly remind employees of their records retention policies (which typically include records disposal guidelines). However, in Arthur Andersen's obstruction of justice trial, the public learned that Andersen had destroyed numerous documents and email messages related to the SEC's ongoing investigation of Enron. In this context, a seemingly innocuous email "reminder" about the company's retention policy was perceived to be a smoking gun.

By the time a jury found Andersen guilty on one count of obstruction of justice in June 2002, the firm had shrunk by 17,000 employees in the U.S. and had lost 30% of its public company clients.[2] After its conviction in June 2002, Andersen is no longer in the auditing business, was fined $500,000, and put on five years of probation—the maximum penalty under the law. (See Chapter 4 for an in-depth discussion of the Andersen case.)

The case of Andersen raises many interesting questions. Could the document destruction have been prevented? Were there flaws in their Information Management program that helped precipitate the company's downfall? What could its leaders and its lawyers have done differently? And, perhaps most importantly, why did the entire company go down, and not just a small group of accused wrongdoers?

The U.S. Congress, for its part, responded to Andersen's conviction and the seemingly endless parade of corporate scandals of the same era by passing new laws and regulations that have sent ripples (or perhaps tidal waves) through corporate America. One of these new laws was the Sarbanes-Oxley Act of 2002, a complex law that addresses many issues that have an impact on Information Management.

> Many companies, of course are retooling to meet the demands of the federal Sarbanes-Oxley Act. As the string of corporate scandals unfolded at companies including Enron Corp. and WorldCom, Inc., Congress moved last year to revamp the way boards and company officials run their business and disclose information.
>
> *How One Firm Uses Strict Governance To Fix Its Troubles,*
> Wall Street Journal, *August 21, 2003*

So began the new era of Information Management. An era where properly managing records and other information have become inextricably linked with corporate accountability and transparency, which in turn has become connected to fiscal health and stock market valuation. An era of new expectations, new regulations, new laws, new technologies, and new challenges.

Information Management Compliance

However, this is not a book about Andersen, Enron, WorldCom, Tyco, ImClone, or any of the other high-profile cases where there have been accusations, charges, and/or convictions for improper use and management of company information (although we will examine some of these and other cases in detail). This is a book about changes in the Information Management landscape, resulting largely from cases like these and dozens of lower-profile cases. Most importantly, it is about how we can learn to avoid similar problems in our own organizations by developing and implementing Information Management Compliance programs that anticipate problems and take advantage of opportunities.

This is a book about approaching all types of Information Management activities with a new methodology, one that adopts the principles, controls, and discipline upon which many corporate compliance programs are built. While the world of records destruction is the starting point for our exploration, the book examines a broad range of Information Management activities that serve both legal and business needs, and are central to your organization's ongoing success.

This is a book about Information Management Compliance (IMC), which involves:

1) Developing Information Management criteria based on legal, regulatory, and business needs; and,

2) Developing and implementing controls designed to ensure compliance with those policies and procedures.

The first six chapters of this book define and explore the concepts of Information Management, Records Management, IMC, and the business and regulatory environments that we operate in today.

In the second part of the book we present the Seven Keys to Information Management Compliance—this is the practical, action-oriented part of the book. These Seven Keys are:

1) Good policies and procedures

2) Executive-level program responsibility

3) Proper delegation of program roles and components

4) Program communication and training

5) Auditing and monitoring to measure program compliance

6) Effective and consistent program enforcement

7) Continuous program improvement

As a model for these Seven Keys, we used a section of the Federal Sentencing Guidelines ("Guidelines").[3] The Guidelines are used by the federal courts to determine the appropriate punishment for individuals and organizations that violate the federal law. For many years, numerous companies have used the Guidelines to build general corporate compliance programs. However, until now, the Guidelines have generally been overlooked as a source of guidance for Information Management. The time has come to apply the compliance methodology outlined by the Guidelines to Information Management.

In this new era, Information Management requires a proactive approach which recognizes that legal protection *and* business value will result from taking a formal, disciplined, visible, funded, and sustained approach—an approach that begins with an understanding of how an organization's Information Management activities are likely to be judged by the courts, regulators, auditors, and its own executives and shareholders.

IMC is about more than making sure information is not destroyed due to the malicious or inadvertent acts of a few employees. Rather, it is a holistic approach that covers many areas of concern, including:

- Storage management

- Privacy

- Business continuity and disaster recovery planning

- Records management

- Information security

- Transaction management

- Application development and integration

- Technology purchasing and acquisition

- System configuration and management

- And many other areas

We wrote this book for a broad range of readers who have an interest in Information Management issues, with a specific focus on readers who have direct or indirect responsibility for making sure that information is properly used and managed in their organizations. The sphere of people who have some responsibility in this area seems to grow every day, now encompassing everyone from the CEO who needs to sign off on financial reports in accordance with Sarbanes-Oxley; to the IT professional wondering how back-up tapes should be managed; to the compliance officer trying to ensure compliance with emerging privacy laws; to the administrative assistant just trying to decide what to do with all the email messages that his boss has asked him to print out and file; to the lawyer guiding the company through troubled legal waters.

Information Management encompasses management, administrative, operational, technological, human resources, Records Management, legal, and many other areas of an organization. The Seven Keys to IMC that we advance are designed to help professionals in each of those areas understand their responsibilities and what they must contribute to their organization's Information Management efforts.

PART 1

Laying the Foundations of Information Management Compliance

Chapter 1:

Why Information Management Matters

In this first chapter we will explore the concept of Information Management, how it has changed over time, and how it relates to other information-based activities across an organization. Understanding the essence of Information Management will lay the foundation for understanding IMC.

Sink or Swim

In 2003, 800 megabytes of new information was created for each man, woman, and child on the earth—with 92% of it stored on magnetic media, primarily hard drives.[4] Businesses worldwide today use more than 300 million desktop computers that together have the capacity to store 150,000 terabytes of information.[5] The number of email messages sent per day will grow from 31 billion in 2002 to 60 billion by 2006.[6] Roughly 250 billion text messages were sent worldwide using wireless devices in 2001,[7] and business users are expected to make up nearly half of the 500 million people that will be using Instant Messaging by 2006.[8]

Information technology has become so commonplace in today's organizations that much of it is taken for granted. Some observers have even suggested that information technology and automation no longer offer "competitive advantage" because each competitor has essentially the same technology and level of automation.

From the largest Enterprise Resource Planning application in use at a corporation with thousands of employees around the globe, to the tiny credit card-size cell phone used by the independent consultant down the street, there are an ever-increasing number of software applications and hardware devices creating an ever-increasing amount of information. Information that must be sent, received, captured, accessed, stored, indexed, published, and so on. Put simply, information that must be managed.

The need for effective Information Management has never been greater.

What Is Information Management?

In the 1970s, the U.S. government commissioned a report that looked at the way government agencies were using information.[9] This report helped to popularize the concept of Information Management. The commission was concerned with both paper and electronic information and the way it was being managed through such diverse activities as library management, microforms, and word processing.

Over the ensuing decades, the term Information Management has come to be used in different ways by a number of groups, as the following definitions illustrate.

Selected Definitions of Information Management

The application of management principles to the acquisition, organization, control, dissemination, and use of information relevant to the effective operation of organizations of all kinds.

'Information' here refers to all types of information of value, whether having their origin inside or outside the organization, including data resources, such as production data; records and files related, for example, to the personnel function; market research data; and competitive intelligence from a wide range of sources. Information management deals with the value, quality, ownership, use, and security of information in the context of organizational performance.

International Encyclopedia of Information and Library Science[10]

■

The proper organization and appropriate control of information transmitted by whatever means and including Records Management.

Comparative Glossary of Common Project Management Terms[11]

■

The administration, use, and transmission of information and the application of theories and techniques of information science to create, modify, or improve information handling systems.

Environmental Protection Agency[12]

■

An imprecise term covering the various stages of information processing from production to storage and retrieval to dissemination towards the better working of an organisation; information can be from internal and external sources and in any format.

The Society for Information Management (UK)[13]

Changing Times, Changing Terms

As business practices and technologies have evolved, so too have the theories about Information Management. Like others working in fields where information technology had provided a radical transformative force, Information Management professionals and their industry groups have worked to stay ahead of the curve.

For example, AIIM International started life in 1943 as the National Microfilm Association, later became the Association for Information and Image Management, and today focuses on enterprise content management (ECM).[14] ECM is a vision of Information Management that refers to several related categories of information technology and processes including:

> content/document management, business process management, enterprise portals, knowledge management, image management, data warehousing, and data mining.[15]

ARMA International, an industry association for Information Management professionals, defines the activities of their members as "recorded information management" (RIM),

> a specialized field of information management that is concerned with the systematic analysis and control of operating records associated with business activities.[16]

ARMA has also theorized that the future of RIM is SIM—Strategic Information Management,

> that body of knowledge comprised of skills that will enable professionals and their organizations to make well-informed decisions resulting in a distinct competitive advantage in the business world. It draws upon skills from records and information management, information technology, and strategic management.[17]

One of the most recent buzzwords in the Information Management world is "information lifecycle management" (ILM), which refers to the use of a combination of procedures and technology to managing an organization's information flow. Like many of the other terms used today, ILM is partly an old concept in a new wrapper, as the "life-cycle" approach to managing information has long been a central tenet of Records Management.

Part of the reason that terms like ILM, RIM, SIM, ECM, information resources management, and even Information Management have been adopted by these communities is a desire to escape the stigma perceived by some to be attached to the term Records Management (RM).

Outside the community of people and organizations responsible for managing records, Records Management is often perceived as a non-strategic cost center. The average employee, or executive for that matter, commonly perceives RM simply as the basement where paper records are stored or part of the mailroom. It is easy to see why such perceptions have made it difficult for many RM departments to gain the visibility and funding they require to perform their corporate function. The relationship between Information Management and Records Management will be discussed further in a later chapter.

An Umbrella Term

Information Management is about determining which information created and received by your organization is valuable in some way, based on its content; making sure that this information is properly protected, stored, shared, and transmitted; and making it easily available to the people who need it, when they need it, and in a format that they can rely on.

Information Management, then, is an umbrella term that includes a variety of disciplines and activities, each focusing on different kinds of information and different kinds of management. In fact, in the broadest sense, Information Management touches on every business activity where information is received or created.

The table below provides some general examples of business activities related to Information Management. Although these activities have separate labels and definitions, in reality there is a great deal of overlap and interdependency amongst them.

Activity	Kinds of Information	Basic Goal
Records management	Business records	Making sure business records are properly retained for legal, compliance, and business purposes, and then properly disposed of when no longer needed
Document management	"Documents" – a wide range of digital information	Ensuring that there are controls in place for the creation and storage of business documents so that they are easily accessible to knowledge workers and others
Knowledge management	Operational information of all kinds	Ensuring that the knowledge of some individuals and groups in an organization is harnessed for use by others in the organization
Enterprise content management	Umbrella term for technologies, tools, and methods used to capture, manage, store, preserve, and deliver content across an enterprise	Often used as a broad term to include activities such as document management, knowledge management, and published content (including website content)
Information security	All valuable information, with a focus on sensitive, confidential, and proprietary information	Ensuring that valuable information is accessible only to those authorized to see it; and ensuring its trustworthiness
Information privacy	Sensitive information, as determined by policy or law, including information about clients, customers, and patients	Ensuring that the collection of and access to sensitive information is properly controlled
Disaster recovery	Information needed to continue business operations	Ensuring that vital information required to operate the business can be recovered in a timely fashion after a disaster
Customer/client relationship management	Information about an organization's interactions with customers/clients and prospects	Ensuring that the customers' experience with a company is satisfactory and consistent; identifying customer patterns that can lead to more revenue
Storage management	All stored digital business information	Ensuring that storage resources such as disk drives and back-up media are used cost-effectively
Data mining	Structured information, such as databases	Providing tools and techniques for collecting and analyzing stored data

The Price of Failure

The price of compliance failures can be huge in both financial and human terms. Failing to follow company policies because of laziness, lack of oversight, or negligence can and does have profound consequences.

For example, in *Murphy Oil USA, Inc. v. Fluor Daniel, Inc*,[18] the court heard a dispute in which Murphy Oil wanted Fluor Daniel to go through nearly 20 million pages of email records to see if any of those records related to the case. The reason there were so many pages of email to search through is that Fluor had apparently not been following its own policy, as the court noted:

"Fluor's email retention policy provided that backup tapes were recycled after 45 days. If Fluor had followed this policy, the email issue would be moot. Fluor does not explain why, but it maintained its backup tapes for the entire 14-month period."

Fluor estimated that the cost of providing relevant documents from the 20 million pages of email and attachments would be in excess of $6 million, and would take six months—far more than the cost would have been if they had followed their own policy.

Cases like these illustrate the need for organizations to develop an accurate estimate of the Total Cost of Failure (TCF) of Information Management Failures. See page 152 for more information on calculating the price of Information Management failures.

Determine Your Needs

Information Management encompasses many different activities, disciplines, people, and—no doubt—departments in your organization. The people responsible for operating the company firewall, for example, are probably in a different part of the building from the people who figure out how the customer relationship management system should work. This is part of the challenge inherent to Information Management—it is difficult to get an overall picture of how your company manages its information.

When examining your Information Management needs, start by getting the "10,000-foot view," and then work down into the details. This will require executive involvement, as we'll explore in Key 2. It will also require research into the activities of various departments throughout your organization.

Make a list of all the activities in your organization that fall under the Information Management umbrella. Since many of these activities center on technology, your IT/IS department may be a good place to start.

For example, find out:

- Who is responsible for each Information Management activity on your list? Does responsibility reside with a Records Management department, a compliance department, the IT/IS department, or a combination of these and others?

- Are there policies and practices that govern each activity? For example, do employees know if they can use the company email system for personal business, and does the webmaster know what kinds of content needs to be approved by the general counsel before being posted on the company website?

- Does your organization use a different term for Information Management that means the same thing? If so, ensure that the term is well understood throughout the company and used consistently.

- Is the Records Management expertise in your company being applied to information technology? In other words, do the Records Management people and the IT people coordinate their activities?

- When was the last time that policies were reviewed to make sure they have kept pace with new laws and regulations that affect your industry? If you haven't reviewed your policies since 2001, for example, you should do so to ensure compliance with the Sarbanes-Oxley Act of 2002.

Chapter 2:

Building the Foundation: Defining Records

Organizations must have a consistent method for determining if informa-
tion is a record and therefore needs to be retained and managed according
to special rules. Determining this can be complex, but as this chapter
explores, there are several guidelines that organizations can use to help.

Determining If Information Is a Record

An organization does not have to retain all information that it creates
or receives. However, internal policies, laws, regulations, standards,
and best practices dictate that certain kinds of information—namely,
records—are retained and managed in a specific way. As such, it is
obviously important that organizations have a method for identifying records.

In the digital world, there are many kinds of electronic documents,
messages, notes, and various other kinds of digital files and other
"stuff" that might or might not be considered a record. If all of this
incredible volume of digital stuff had to be captured and managed,
most businesses would be overwhelmed or even crushed beneath the
weight. However, to make it even more difficult, getting rid of the
wrong information can have severe legal consequences.

It quickly becomes apparent that an organization needs a way to
determine which information it should retain as a record, and which

information can be discarded. In order to do this, organizations must first define and understand the function of records.

Quiz Time: Which Digital Information Might Need to Be Retained?

- "Clicks" on your company's Web page regarding customer purchases?

- Mass voicemail messages to customers about a new product offering?

- Employee 401K plan selections made via a telephone keypad on your company's Interactive Voice Response (IVR) telephone system?

- Voicemail from a regulator asking questions about a mandatory filing?

- An Instant Message from a business partner agreeing to pay half the marketing costs of a new product initiative?

If you answered yes to all of the above, you are correct. The fact that the above information exists in digital form, and may appear more casual or ephemeral than information in paper or other form does not diminish your organization's obligation to retain information that has business, operational, legal, regulatory, and/or historical significance.

Defining Records

Selected Definitions of Record

A written account of some act, court proceeding, transaction, or instrument, drawn up, under authority of law, by proper officer, and designed to remain as a memorial or permanent evidence of the matters to which it relates.

Black's Law Dictionary

Information created, received and maintained as evidence and information by an organization, or person, in pursuance of legal obligations or in the transaction of business.

ISO[19]

■

All books, papers, maps, photographs, machine readable materials, or other documentary materials, regardless of physical form or characteristics, made or received by an agency of the United States Government under Federal law or in connection with the transaction of public business and preserved or appropriate for preservation by that agency or its legitimate successor as evidence of the organization, functions, policies, decisions, procedures, operations, or other activities of the Government or because of the informational value of data in them. Library and museum material made or acquired and preserved solely for reference or exhibition purposes, extra copies of documents preserved only for convenience of reference, and stocks of publications and of processed documents are not included.

U.S. federal law (44 U.S.C. 3301), the definition also used by the U.S. National Archives and Records Administration, or NARA

Although each of these definitions takes a different approach to defining the term "record," there is also a great deal of commonality here. Each emphasizes the idea that a record must actually be *recorded* in some way, whether as a "writing" as described by the law dictionary, or as "machine readable materials" as described in the definition used by NARA. Similarly, the definitions make clear that the purpose of a record is to serve as evidence of something, such as a "court proceeding" in the case of the Black's definition, or "the transaction of business," as defined by ISO.

It is instructive to note that the more recently created (in the case of the ISO definition) and specific (in the case of the federal government definition) definitions make clear that records serve both a legal *and* a business purpose. The focus on records as *business* evidence represents an ongoing shift that has been occurring in the Information Management world for some time, as organizations have come to realize how fundamental information has become to their operations. After all, in the "information age," where capturing, managing, and using information has become a central business activity in most large organizations, the business purpose of records and other information is self-evident.

Why These Definitions Matter

Recently in our consulting practice, while performing a final review of email retention guidelines we had drafted for a client, we noticed that the definition of "record" had been changed by our client, who had added the following statement to the draft:

> A Record is inscribed on a tangible medium and, as such, is retrievable in a viewable form.

We reminded the client's attorney that there were in fact many records in use at their company that did not fit the new definition. These included interactive voice response records, audiotapes of meetings, and other records that are indeed "inscribed on a tangible medium," but are not "retrievable in viewable form." The definition needed to be changed.

There is currently no definition of "record" that is universally used by all organizations, and for good reason. Definitions serve the community that they are created by, and each community has different needs. There is no reason why your organization's definition of "record" needs to strictly conform to other organizations in your industry. However, it only makes sense to leverage the work that organizations such as ISO, for example, have done when defining records. The key characteristic of a good definition for your purposes is that it is broad enough to encompass all the information you need to retain for business, operational, legal, regulatory, and/or historical purposes, without being so broad that employees cannot understand or apply it in practice.

Our definition of "record" below is the one that we often use in our consulting practice, and encompasses key records concepts:

A record is information recorded on a tangible medium (paper or electronic media being two common examples) and intentionally retained and managed as evidence of an organization's activities, events, or transactions for business, operational, legal, regulatory, and/or historical purposes.

See page 33 for an example of the business, operational, and regulatory purposes that records fulfill.

Defining "Business Information"

When drafting policies and discussing Information Management issues, there are many occasions where it is necessary to broadly refer to all information related to an organization's business operations, whether or not that information qualifies as a record and is retained and managed according to record retention rules. This is necessary, for example, when discussing ownership of information assets in Information Management policies (see page 103 for more information).

Many organizations use the term "business information." Our baseline definition for "business information," which we customize according to the type of client, is:

> Information generated or received by the company or its employees and used in the operation of our business. Business information includes records, data, and documents stored in any form (e.g., paper, electronic, audio and video recordings, and imaging media).

Why We Retain Records

Records are central to every organization's ability to operate its business. Without a consistent way to identify and manage records, and to properly dispose of unneeded information, the following functions of records will be threatened:

- To serve customers (e.g., by providing timely access to accurate purchasing info)

- To plan and forecast (e.g., by consulting records of past sales performance)

- To serve as an "organizational memory" (e.g., corporate archives and libraries)

- To meet legal obligations (e.g., tax laws)

- To protect legal and business interests (e.g., contracts)

- To comply with regulations (e.g., health, safety, and environmental laws)

- To satisfy the courts (e.g., retaining records subject to subpoena)

- To help resolve disagreements and disputes (e.g., regarding agreements, promises, claims, or representations)

The ability to properly and consistently retain business records is especially important today, as more and more records are in electronic form—a form that makes it much easier to lose, alter, disseminate, replicate, or improperly dispose of records (a topic explored in detail throughout this book).

Is It "Just Data," or Is It a Record?

Too many organizations make the mistake of viewing the output of IT systems, the contents of databases, data streams, and other electronic information as "just data" that has limited value to their organizations. However, before being so quick to pass judgment on this digital information, ask yourself the following questions—that "data" may be more important than you think:

- Does it document a business activity?

- Does the information have business, operational, legal, regulatory, and/or historic value to the company?

- If it were in paper form, would it be retained?

- Does the law expect that your organization will retain it?

- Could it help resolve a dispute in the future?

Not All Information Has to Be Retained

[W]e see no evidence of fraud or bad faith in a corporation destroying records if it is no longer required by law to keep and which are destroyed in accord with its regular practices. As we have previously observed, storage of records for big or small businesses is a costly item and destruction of records no longer required is not in and of itself evidence of spoliation.

Moore v. General Motors[20]

As the quote above demonstrates, the courts have made clear that organizations do not have to retain all the information that they create or receive, nor do they have to retain all records indefinitely. In fact, a key benefit of developing a consistent method for identifying and managing records is that it allows organizations to get rid of unneeded information and records without fear of legal sanctions. This has the additional benefit of reducing the burden on precious enterprise storage resources that are already under the strain of volumes of email messages, Instant Messages, documents, spreadsheets, and so on.

Top 10 Reasons NOT to Keep Everything Forever:

1) The law does not require it.

2) Only increases the risk of outdated documents being exposed that can damage the company's legal position.

3) May require maintenance of expensive "legacy" software and hardware to recreate original content years after it was created.

4) Aged storage media needs to be refreshed and data migrated to ensure continued access—an expensive and time-consuming process.

5) Data tends to grow exponentially, making it increasingly difficult to retrieve what you are looking for.

6) Costs associated with discovery in litigation increase with the volume of data that must be reviewed.

7) Purchasing, managing, maintaining, and migrating excess storage media is expensive.

8) Many business processes, from serving customers to forecasting sales, are slower and less effective when systems are bogged down with useless information.

9) Makes it harder to respond quickly to regulators and courts, either of which can dictate fast turnaround times for providing specific information.

10) Makes it impractical and cost-prohibitive to apply controls and technology to information that requires special handling, such as private customer data.

Medium Does Not Matter

Imagine that you receive the following memo:

> ATTN: All Employees
>
> RE: Corporate Efficiency
>
> The Executive Records Management Committee has decided that in order to save money and cut down on office clutter, we will be destroying all files that reside in gray filing cabinets. Consequently, we request that all employees IMMEDIATELY remove all files in gray filing cabinets in their vicinity and place them in industrial shredders that will be provided.
>
> Only gray filing cabinets are affected by this directive. Blue and tan filing cabinets are exempt. Thank your for your cooperation.
>
> Executive Records Management Committee

The thinking behind such a memo would be mystifying. How could the company get away with destroying files without any regard to their content, just because they reside in gray filing cabinets?

This obviously would never happen in the paper world, but it happens all the time in the digital world. Organizations routinely purge their enterprise email systems every 30, 60, or 90 days without regard for the value of the information that is contained in those purged email messages. Not only does this approach eliminate the potential benefits of harnessing the knowledge that is captured in the email system, but the company may also open itself up to serious legal consequences as a result of this practice.

How can the company assume that the email system does not contain records simply because the medium is email? Indiscriminately purging an entire email system after a short period of time and without regard to the content is just like indiscriminately purging paper files that are housed in gray filing cabinets.

The lesson here is that the medium does not matter when deciding whether or not information qualifies as a record. Email systems, text messaging services, voicemail systems, and peer-to-peer networks are all just transmission vehicles for information that may or may not be a record. In other words, the method used to send, create, or receive information, and the medium used to store information, do not matter when determining if certain content qualifies as a record. The laws usually do not differentiate when it comes to medium, and neither should your organization.

Intent Does Matter

Our definition of record on (see page 21) states that a record is "intentionally retained and managed as evidence of an organization's activities, events, or transactions."

Intent provides a key to determining if a specific piece of information is in fact a record. Although this can be challenging in the paper world, it is even harder in the digital world, where multiple copies of an email message and its attachments can exist on several computers around the globe at the same time. Assuming a particular email message qualifies as a business record, which copy (or copies) of the email must be retained and managed?

Let's look at a case where a word processing document is passed amongst several colleagues via email, each person adding comments and revisions along the way. Each employee has now saved several copies and versions of the document in his or her file system, and all those versions are saved on the central email server.

Which copy of this document should be retained as the record? If the company's Records Management policy states that only the final version of this type of document must be captured and retained in a central Records Management system, then the final version of the document is the record, and all other copies can be safely deleted, barring any law or regulation to the contrary.[21]

In other words, the company has made clear, through its policy and actions, that the final version is intended to be the "official" record. Intent is the key.

Intent is critical because digital information has qualities that can make it difficult to determine which copy of a file is the official record. These qualities include:

- The ability to make infinite perfect copies of an electronic file

- The ease of instantly disseminating perfect copies to people around the globe at the touch of key

- The difficulty of tracking versions of the same file without special software

- The ease of altering a digital file, both inadvertently and intentionally

In general, only the "official" version of a record needs to be retained and managed.

Determining which copy of a digital file is the official record is important for a variety of reasons. First, barring any legal reason to the contrary, it allows organizations to retain a single copy of a file and discard the rest with legal comfort, resulting in storage cost savings. Second, it reduces the chance that courts will make an organization search through gigabytes of data for all copies of a file in the course of discovery in a trial or investigation (more on this later). Third, it makes it easier for employees to properly retain records of their work.

Let's look at another example involving a file disseminated by email among colleagues. If you send an important email message (which qualifies as a record) to Tom, and send copies (using the cc: address field) to Dick and Harry as well, now there are four copies of the email message in existence (plus copies on the central email server). Is one of them an official record that must be retained and managed?

Different organizations might answer this question differently. As a matter of policy, many would say that only Tom (the person to whom the email was sent directly), and not Dick or Harry (the cc'ed parties), need to retain a copy of the email for recordkeeping purposes. So, the direct recipient's copy of the email would be the only official record, as it is the one retained for recordkeeping purposes; the other copies can be disposed of because an official record has been designated and retained.

However, there are many subtleties to this issue. Some organizations may only require the sender to retain the message, while others may require anyone who is required to take action as a result of the email message, regardless of whether or not they are the direct recipient to retain a copy. The right answer for your organization derives from a combination of its organizational culture, technical capabilities, regulatory environment, and litigation history.

What is certain is that all organizations must ensure that procedures for designating and retaining "official records" are formally documented, widely disseminated, and properly understood and enforced—as with any other Information Management policy or procedure. Doing so establishes your organization's intent to capture, retain, and manage specific copies or versions of records as official records. Formally establishing this intent reduces the likelihood that a court, regulator, auditor, or other outside party will take issue with the disposition of non-official records.

The Business Records Exception to the Hearsay Rule

When the courts consider evidence in a case, they typically prefer to have testimony from individuals who have direct, first-hand knowledge of the matter at hand—for example, an eyewitness, a party to the conversation in question, or someone involved in the creation of a document or record. This type of testimony is generally thought most likely to be trustworthy and accurate. In most cases, non-direct, second-hand testimony is considered to be "hearsay" and cannot be admitted as evidence.

Business records are considered to be a form of hearsay, but are generally allowable under the "business records" exception to the hearsay rule. This exception is described in the Federal Rules of Evidence (FRE), a set of rules for how evidence is handled in federal courts. Among other things, the FRE require that the business records must have been "kept in the course of a regularly conducted business," and "the source of information or the method or circumstances of preparation" must be trustworthy.[22]

Record Qualification Checklist

Here is a checklist to help you apply the definition of a record to the information within your organization. This list is not exhaustive, but represents a sampling of criteria.

It is probably a record if:

- A regulation or statute says it must be retained

- It contains valuable information about business operations

- It contains information that must be filed with a regulator

- It is an Instant Message that was used to negotiate a contract

- It is a voicemail message from a regulator about official business

- The sales forecast depends on information it contains

- It is the final version of a contract

- It has business, compliance, historical, operational, and/or legal value or significance to the organization

Survey: Employee Responsibility for Records and Information

1) Does the company provide employees with retention rules for electronic records?

2) Does the company provide guidance and training for all employees on what information can be sent across the Internet?

3) Do all employees receive training on their Records Management responsibilities as part of their new employee orientation?

4) Does the company provide specific rules about how and where to retain email records that require long-term retention?

5) Are employees provided with any technological solutions or tools to secure laptops, PDAs, or other handheld computers?

If you answered "No" to any of the above, your organization likely has more work to do to get the employees engaged in helping to manage its information assets.

Chapter 3:

An Overview of Records Management

In Chapter 1, we explored how diverse Information Management activities fit together. In Chapter 2, we defined "record" and examined the need for organizations to properly identify and retain business records. In this chapter we will look in detail at the systematic management of records (i.e., Records Management) and examine how Records and Information Management fit together.

Defining Records Management

Information Management is a broad category of activities, all of which must be carried out with a view to compliance. For example, it is just as important that an organization's information security policies reflect current laws as it is for a customer relationship management application to protect customer privacy. Both areas are part of Information Management, and both must be compliant with relevant criteria.

In many ways, however, Records Management is not just another activity under the umbrella of Information Management. In fact, Records Management typically deals with the most sensitive, valuable, and challenging information in an organization. This is why we have chosen to devote an entire chapter to the topic.

Whereas Information Management is a broad activity encompassing many different types of information and management activities, Records Management focuses on a particular type of information, namely records. In this sense, Records Management is a subset or component of Information Management. Records Management is a complex topic, and the purpose of this chapter is not to provide an exhaustive overview of it, but rather to highlight key issues that relate to IMC.

As the definitions below demonstrate, there are many different takes on Records Management. However, each of the definitions makes clear that Records Management is focused on the formal and systematic management of important information from the time it is "born" to the time it no longer serves a purpose within an organization and is disposed.

Selected Definitions of Records Management

Field of management responsible for the efficient and systematic control of the creation, receipt, maintenance, use and disposition of records, including processes for capturing and maintaining evidence of and information about business activities and transactions in the form of records.

ISO[23]

■

From the Federal perspective, it is the planning, controlling, directing, organizing, training, promoting, and other managerial activities involved in records creation, maintenance and use, and disposition in order to achieve adequate and proper documentation of the policies and transactions of the Federal Government (36 CFR 1220.14).

NARA (U.S. National Archives and Records Administration)[24]

■

"The planning, controlling, directing, organizing, training, promoting, and other managerial activities involving the lifecycle of information, including creation, maintenance (use, storage, retrieval), and disposal, regardless of media."

U.S. Department of Defense[25]

The Lifecycle Approach

Contemporary Records Management is largely based on what is commonly known as a "lifecycle." Information is viewed as having a lifecycle with a beginning, middle, and end—much like any living organism. However, a record's lifecycle isn't so much natural as it is imposed through a Records Management program. Borrowing from the U.S. Department of Defense definition above, we can say that this lifecycle goes through the following stages:

1) Creation

2) Use

3) Storage

4) Retrieval

5) Disposal

There are other ways to break down the various stages in the lifecycle, but put simply, the lifecycle includes everything that happens to a record from the time it is created until the time that it is disposed of.

Information Assets

The lifecycle approach is valuable because it enables organizations to perceive business records as assets with value that changes over time—just like any other asset. That is why records and other business information are often referred to as "information assets."

Take, for example, a potential customer submitting a request for information about a new drug through a form on a pharmaceutical company's website. In this example, the information contained in the customer request serves several purposes throughout its lifecycle, especially these three:

1) **Business purpose.** First, the information in the customer's request is required simply for the purposes of responding appropriately. The request details what the customer wants and enables the company representative to craft a useful response. In this sense, the record serves a clear business

purpose. If the request were somehow lost, altered, or disposed of before the representative could generate a response, then a potential business opportunity would be lost.

2) **Operational purpose.** Once the customer has been satisfied, there may be many operational purposes for the information. For example, the company could keep track of how many customers have requested information in order to gauge the success of marketing programs. Or the company could keep track of how many times customers ask the same questions, and if justified, create a simple FAQ, automated response, or perhaps a more detailed, searchable "knowledge base" about this particular product, as many companies do. In these examples, the objective at this stage in the information lifecycle is to provide information that can be used for business planning, customer relationship management, and other operational purposes.

3) **Regulatory purposes.** Depending on the nature of the information request, the pharmaceutical company may have an obligation to retain a record of the customer exchange according to Food and Drug Administration regulations. In this case, managing the record helps the company comply with the law and protects it from other legal problems that may arise.

This simple example demonstrates some of the roles that records play throughout their lifecycle. Although the purpose of the records and the source of its value may change over time, the need to properly retain and manage the record does not.

Components of a Records Management Program

The makeup of Records Management programs varies from organization to organization according to size, the nature of their business activities, organizational culture, regulatory environment, and several other factors. Records Management programs range from very formal, broad programs with dedicated departments and dozens of employees, to informal programs that are run by an administrator on an ad hoc basis.

Despite this variability, there are several fundamental components that every Records Management program should consist of to be adequate, effective, and efficient.

The U.S. Environmental Protection Agency (EPA) definition of a Records Management program provides a useful overview of its basic elements.

According to the EPA, a Records Management program is:

> A planned, coordinated set of policies, procedures, and activities needed to manage an agency's recorded information. Encompasses the creation, maintenance and use, and disposition of records, regardless of media. Essential elements include issuing up-to-date program directives, properly training those responsible for implementation, publicizing the program, and carefully evaluating the results to ensure adequacy, effectiveness, and efficiency.[26]

By breaking this definition down and paraphrasing it, we can identify the critical elements of a Records Management program:

A Records Management program is a planned, coordinated set of policies, procedures, and activities designed to manage recorded information through its lifecycle, regardless of the media upon which it is recorded. Essential elements include:

- Up-to-date program directives

- Proper training to ensure thorough implementation

- Building organizational awareness of the program

- Auditing the program for adequacy, effectiveness, and efficiency

Additional components of successful Records Management programs are listed below, and are explored in greater detail throughout the book.

- A comprehensive body of policies, procedures, and implementation guidelines dealing with issues of record creation, what to retain, where, by whom, classification, ownership of records, security, disposition, and so on

- Completion of a records inventory and other information gathering to determine what records are in use and the reason for their use so that laws and regulations can be consulted about periods of retention

- Retention rules (based on legal requirements, legal considerations, and business needs) that tell employees how long to retain various categories of records

- A Records Management organization with sufficient support, visibility, accountability, budget, and staff to fulfill the goals of the Records Management program

- A formal process (often called a "Records or Legal Hold") for finding, preserving, and producing records and other tangible evidence in the context of expected or current litigation, audits, investigations, and other formal proceedings

- A comprehensive training program for all employees to ensure they understand their Records Management responsibilities and how to fulfill them

- Special rules for managing and retaining email and other types of electronic records, as required

- Special rules for handling special records, such as Vital, Privileged, Trade Secret, and Private records

- An auditing or review mechanism to ensure that employees are doing what they are supposed to regarding the management of records

Managing Electronic Records

Electronic records (e-records) can be used in place of paper records for more purposes and in more jurisdictions than ever before. E-records can also be offered as evidence in most jurisdictions without concern that they will be deemed "inadmissible" merely because they are not in paper form, or because they are not "an original." The federal E-SIGN Act, for example, clarifies that "a signature, contract, or other record… may not be denied legal effect, validity, or enforceability solely because it is in electronic form."[27] Cases such as *U.S. v. Catabran* make clear that "it is immaterial that the business record is maintained in a computer rather than in company books," for the purposes of admissibility.[28]

Laws regarding electronic information and records generally address what is acceptable to the courts, what is acceptable to regulators and government agencies, or both. At the same time, these laws and regulations typically take the approach of either allowing the use of electronic information for legal and regulatory purposes, or of stipulating specific requirements designed to ensure that electronic records and evidence are trustworthy, complete, reliable, secure, and so on. Laws and regulations, even those that provide specific criteria, tend to be technology-neutral. That is, they do not require the use of particular technology.

Electronic Records Must Be Trustworthy

At the same time, organizations need to be aware that just because electronic records and information can be relied upon in more situations than ever before, courts and regulators still expect electronic records to be trustworthy.

Trustworthy records are the product of informed and committed efforts to properly manage them. Building good electronic records begins with an understanding of what makes them trustworthy.

Trustworthiness is most accurately thought of as a quality that results from the sum total of the people, procedures, environments, strategies, and technologies used throughout the lifecycle of a business record. Trustworthiness suggests that a court, regulator, or auditor—and the organization itself—can trust and rely upon the content of a record.

A trustworthy electronic record has four key qualities, including:

1) **Integrity.** An e-record has integrity if it can be demonstrated that its contents have not been altered since the e-record was created, and that the record remained complete from its creation to disposition.

2) **Accuracy.** An e-record is accurate if it contains the information it is supposed to contain, as originally intended, and the content remains the same over its entire lifecycle.

3) **Authenticity.** An e-record is said to be authentic if it is in fact "what it purports to be." That is, the source or origin of the e-record can be reliably demonstrated. This often requires proof of who generated an e-record, and who controlled it over its lifecycle (often called an "audit trail").

4) **Accessibility**. Trustworthiness implies that an organization or an outside party will be able to rely on an e-record for business, legal, or compliance purposes. A record that cannot be accessed in a timely fashion during its lifecycle precludes its use for these purposes. Accessibility can be threatened by poor indexing, the finite life span of storage media, hardware obsolescence, software incompatibility, environmental degradation, and many other factors.

Digital Trustworthiness Is a Challenge

Regulators demand that standards of information integrity and accuracy must be met. The courts have excluded electronic evidence that they have deemed untrustworthy. In addition, it does an organization little good to expend the resources necessary to manage e-records if the organization itself cannot be sure of their integrity. As such, the issue of trustworthiness is more than just a legal issue—it is central to an organization's ability to plan, strategize, and operate its business.

While the issue of trustworthiness may seem self explanatory when dealing with paper records, e-records have several unique characteristics that make their management challenging. These qualities include:

1) **Complexity.** Understanding the creation of a paper record is usually straightforward. Many e-records, however, are created using complex technological processes that may be hard to explain to a court or regulator, which can add to the time and expense of presenting complex electronic evidence.

2) **Portability.** E-records can be easily created and distributed, which can make it more difficult to track their origin and use throughout their life span.

3) **Alterability.** Unlike the physical bond of ink on paper, most e-records provide no such inherent characteristics that prevent their inadvertent or deliberate alteration—even though certain storage technologies can prohibit unauthorized alteration or deletion.

4) **Hardware and Software.** E-records rely on hardware and software for their display and use—hardware and software that may not always be available.

5) **Multiple Parts.** Paper records contain all of their information within the "four corners" of a document. E-records, on the other hand, can contain metadata and exist in multiple parts in multiple locations—thus making their capture, retrieval, and presentation more problematic.

Excluding Electronic Evidence

The courts can and will exclude (or minimize the evidentiary value of) unauthenticated evidence or evidence that is otherwise deemed to be untrustworthy, as the selection of cases below demonstrates:

Monotype v. International Typeface—email evidence supporting the defendant's case was excluded.[29]

Pettiford v. N.C. HHS—the plaintiff's failure to properly authenticate email messages offered as evidence resulted in the court refusing to consider them as evidence, even though they supported her claim.[30]

Sea-Land Serv. v. Lozen Int'l—unauthenticated electronic evidence was also excluded.[31]

Gamber-Johnson v. Trans Data Net Corp—the court excluded evidence regarding a contractual dispute, which contributed to the court awarding damages for breach of contract to the plaintiff.[32]

There have been many more cases where electronic evidence was excluded, or its persuasiveness in the courtroom was diminished, because the evidence could not be adequately authenticated.

Technology Can Help with Trustworthiness

Although laws and regulations regarding electronic records and digital information are generally technology-neutral, many of these laws and regulations also recognize that the functionality and configuration of software and hardware plays a large role in digital trustworthiness. While these laws and regulations may not describe a specific kind of technology, they do specify functional criteria that must be met by technology used in the management, storage, and retention of required records. These laws and regulations recognize that not all technology is created equal when it comes to ensuring the trustworthiness of electronic records. It is important that your organization also recognizes this fact when selecting and implementing technology for storing and managing electronic records.

One of the clearest examples of this type of regulation is 17 CFR §240.17a-4, a rule promulgated by the SEC addressing records retention and management requirements for broker-dealers. Since 1997, 17a-4 has allowed broker-dealers to retain required records in electronic form, provided that certain requirements are met.

One of these requirements is that the electronic storage media used "[p]reserve the records exclusively in a non-rewriteable, non-erasable format."[33] The SEC has stated that this requirement "is designed to ensure that electronic records are capable of being accurately reproduced for later reference by maintaining the records in unalterable form."[34]

The SEC has clarified that a number of storage technologies and techniques may be used to fulfill this requirement of the regulation, including storage media (such as certain kinds of optical discs and magnetic tape) that offers write-once, read-many (WORM) functionality, or "an electronic storage system that prevents the overwriting, erasing, or otherwise altering of a record during its required retention period through the use of integrated hardware and software control codes."[35]

The key element of the storage system used to comply with the regulation is that it must protect the integrity, accuracy, authenticity, and accessibility of electronic records—the four elements of electronic record trustworthiness outlined above.

Proper technology selection and implementation is important in all facets of IMC, from protecting privacy through encryption and database security, to building intranet-based applications in a way that enables trustworthy records to be captured and retained. This concept is explored in more detail throughout the book.

Chapter 4:

Information Management Compliance (IMC)

In the first three chapters we provided a framework for understanding Information Management and for identifying and managing business records. In this chapter we begin to explore the core concept of the book, Information Management Compliance (IMC).

What Is Compliance?

Although the term compliance is most often associated with the legal world, understanding it solely as a legal term is too narrow. In a broader context, and in the context used in this book, compliance simply means to act in accordance with any accepted standard or criteria. The "accepted standard" can refer to any kind of criteria, including business goals, performance measurements, laws, regulations, or quality targets.

In a general sense, there are two basic elements to compliance, namely:

1) Determining what the criteria should be; and,

2) Developing techniques (often called "controls") to ensure that the criteria are followed.

Compliance is also a specific discipline that is practiced within dedicated departments in many regulated organizations around the world.

These departments focus on ensuring that the organization complies with laws, regulations, codes, and other sources of compliance criteria. According to the International Compliance Association, organizational compliance departments have five key functions:[36]

1) To identify the risks that an organization faces and provide guidance on the identified risks;

2) To design and implement controls to protect an organization from those risks;

3) To monitor and report on the effectiveness of those controls;

4) To resolve compliance difficulties; and,

5) To advise the organization on risks, rules, and controls.

How Compliance and Information Management Fit Together

Although the compliance concept can apply to nearly any activity or department, in this book we are concerned with how to achieve compliance in Information Management.

IMC involves:

1) The development of Information Management criteria based on legal, regulatory, and business needs; and,

2) The implementation of controls designed to ensure compliance with those criteria.

To put it another way, IMC is a fusion of the Compliance discipline with Information Management activities. Although it may seem natural on one level to bring these two areas together, at most organizations Compliance and Information Management typically exist within different departments and exhibit very different cultures. Also, they often take fundamentally different approaches to the problem they are designed to address. That is, Information Management programs often take a "best practices" approach, while Compliance often is based on a "risk management" methodology.

Combining the Two Approaches

As each of those two approaches has strengths and limitations, organizations should employ the best of both in developing their IMC programs.

Information Management programs are typically developed with the objective of achieving a reasonable level of assurance that information will be effectively managed, with a minimum of overhead. Organizations try to achieve that objective by implementing a series of recommendations and practices that are generally accepted as highly effective yet not inordinately costly—commonly called "best practices."

A weakness with this approach is that there really is no single set of best practices that is applicable to all organizations. Further, changes in the economy, operating environment, and technology can make current best practices obsolete.

On the other hand, Compliance tends to take a risk management-based approach. This approach involves identifying the risks that an organization faces; evaluating the potential for damage represented by each risk; and addressing these potentials in a systematic manner.

Common risk factors that an organization typically evaluates when building Compliance programs include:

- The nature and complexity of its business
- The diversity of its operations
- The scale, volume, and value of its business transactions
- The quantities or kinds of litigation
- Regulatory environment and oversight
- The nature and magnitude of risk-related activities

Risk management has its own pitfalls, as it depends not only upon the ability of the organization to identify all possible risks, but to also gauge the likelihood that a particular risk will occur and how often, and determine the appropriate amount of time and energy that should be spent protecting against each risk. Making these judgments and calculations can be very difficult, particularly when addressing "soft" risks such as the chance that a company executive is going to indiscriminately destroy documents related to a trial. In addition, calculating the costs of efforts designed to prevent such eventualities, such as training programs and investments in "corporate culture" is also difficult. See the discussion of Total Cost of Failure (TCF) on page 152 for more information on calculating these costs.

This characterization of Information Management and Compliance is intentionally simplistic, and does not capture the complex mix of strategies that most organizations employ in their Information Management and Compliance programs. The intent is to illustrate the need for organizations to use both best practice and risk management strategies in the development of their Information Management programs.

The process of IMC starts with a body of best practices, and continues by adapting these practices to an organization's specific needs according to their unique legal, regulatory, business, and risk environment.

Sources of IMC Criteria

In Information Management, there are two broad categories of compliance criteria:

1) Criteria imposed on an organization from an external source such as a regulatory body. These include the following criteria:

   ■ **Laws**, such as Sarbanes-Oxley;

   ■ **Regulations**, such as IRS and SEC Rules; and,

   ■ **Industry standards** required by agreement or contract, such as ISO standards that must be followed when manufacturing products for export.

2) Criteria voluntarily adopted or developed by an organization **internally**. These include such criteria as:

- **Methods** developed internally or by industry associations, such as Total Quality Management™ or Six Sigma™, which companies adopt in order to improve internal operations.

- **Voluntary standards and codes** such as website accessibility standards for people with disabilities, published by the World Wide Web Consortium.

- **Operating procedures** developed and refined by an organization over its operating life because they are the most efficient, reflect the company's values, or simply because "that's the way we do things."

Establishing Your Compliance Criteria

Determining all of the criteria that your organization should (or must) comply with can be complex, especially if your organization is international (or subject to multiple jurisdictions) or is involved in many different lines-of-business. The following chart shows some common examples of compliance criteria and the organizations that they affect.

Type of Organization	Sources of Compliance Criteria
Commercial entities	Federal, state, and local laws and statutes governing business operations, such as tax laws and commercial codes
Government agencies	Government standards for performance, accountability, and reporting, such as those created by the U.S. Office of Management and Budget (OMB)
Public companies	Federal, state, and local laws governing the conduct of public companies, such as the Sarbanes-Oxley Act
Manufacturing companies	ISO 9000 series standards regarding manufacturing practices
Companies online	Web "privacy seals" such as TRUSTe, and privacy standards such as the Platform for Privacy Preferences, promulgated by the World Wide Web Consortium
Information technology companies	Technical standards, such as Department of Defense standards for electronic recordkeeping systems; and quality standards for suppliers to pharmaceutical companies

Compliance Is a Process, Not a Project

Implementing new technology that has Information Management significance requires close attention to the ongoing compliance of the technology with criteria that support the goals of your Information Management program.

For example, many organizations embarking upon imaging projects (i.e., converting paper records to digital images) discover that there is far more to scanning and imaging than meets the eye. In fact, if done properly, the process may consist of numerous stand-alone activities—from proper document preparation, to the development of a comprehensible indexing regime, to a post-scan review to ensure complete capture and usability of the image. To get it right, organizations need to develop policies and procedures based on industry best practices or standards. These policies become the "compliance criteria" for making sure that employees know what to do to get it right every time, at every step of the process.

Thereafter, organizations must ensure that employees continue to get it right. Continued vigilance may require monitoring the actions of the employees; auditing to ensure that the captured images are of a high quality; and retraining employees regularly.

If organizations think that the "imaging project" is over when the technology "goes live," they need to think again, because this attitude will likely mean an IMC breakdown is in their future.

In other words, compliance is a process, not a project.

Organizational Liability

A corporation can only act through natural persons, and it is therefore held responsible for the acts of such persons fairly attributable to it. Charging a corporation for even minor misconduct may be appropriate where the wrongdoing was pervasive and was undertaken by a large number of employees or by all the employees in a particular role within the corporation... or was condoned by upper management.

On the other hand, in certain limited circumstances, it may not be appropriate to impose liability upon a corporation, particularly one with a compliance program in place, under a strict respondeat superior theory for the single isolated act of a rogue employee. There is, of course, a wide spectrum between these two extremes, and a prosecutor should exercise sound discretion in evaluating the pervasiveness of wrongdoing within a corporation.

Federal Prosecution of Business Organizations, U.S. Department of Justice[37]

Organizations, as well as individuals, can be tried and convicted for breaking the law. There are many reasons why an organization could be found liable. In many cases, a company is taken to task because it failed to employ adequate policies, supervision, training, discipline, corrective action, or other controls designed to diminish the likelihood of wrongdoing. In these cases the problem is seen to be so systemic that the organization must be punished in order to provide restitution to those damaged by its failure, and to ensure that its practices change.

A legal principle or "doctrine" called "*respondeat superior*" is commonly used by the courts to determine whether or not an organization should be held liable for the illegal acts performed by, or the damages caused by, its employees. Under this doctrine, an organization can be held "vicariously liable," providing that an employee's actions "(i) were within the scope of his duties and (ii) were intended, at least in part, to benefit the corporation."[38] Many cases where organizations were held liable for the Information Management failures and bad acts of its employees are explored throughout this book.

When federal prosecutors are faced with fraud and other criminal activity within corporations, they consider a number of factors when deciding whether to prosecute the corporation in addition to the individuals directly responsible for the wrongdoing.

These factors, which are provided in a manual for U.S. federal prosecutors (quoted above),[39] include:

1) The nature and seriousness of the offense

2) The pervasiveness of wrongdoing within the corporation, including the complicity in, or condoning of, the wrongdoing by corporate management

3) The corporation's history of similar conduct

4) The corporation's timely and voluntary disclosure of wrongdoing and its willingness to cooperate in the investigation of its agents

5) The existence and adequacy of the corporation's compliance program

6) The corporation's remedial actions

7) Collateral consequences, including disproportionate harm to shareholders and employees not proven personally culpable

8) The adequacy of the prosecution of individuals responsible for the corporation's malfeasance

9) The adequacy of remedies such as civil or regulatory enforcement actions

A Case Study in IMC Failure: The Enron/Andersen Case

Andersen's conduct in obstructing the Securities and Exchange Commission investigation of Enron, we submit, contributed to—contributed to significantly—the historic shaking of the foundations of our markets.

Samuel W. Buell, federal prosecutor in the Andersen trial[40]

There are a number of IMC lessons to be learned from the Enron/Andersen case. Although the story of Andersen's demise is far from the only case where Information Management Compliance failures have had disastrous consequences, the sheer magnitude of the consequences of their IMC failures was unprecedented—Andersen went from being one of the world's most respected companies to virtual non-existence nearly overnight.

That being said, as with any case like Andersen's, there are complex legal issues at play, varying accounts of what occurred and why, and differing opinions on the outcome. The intention of discussing Andersen here is not to examine those specific issues, but rather to explore the lessons that can be learned and used by all organizations when building and implementing their Information Management programs.

By the time Andersen was convicted in June 2002 of obstructing the SEC's investigation into its auditing of Enron, Andersen's auditing business had been substantially impacted. Many of the company's auditing clients had already dropped the firm when it was indicted about four months earlier. Clearly, many of the company's clients must have believed, as apparently did the prosecutors, that the problems at Andersen were systemic—and not merely the result of a few "bad eggs."

> Today's hearing will explore how one of the world's premiere professional organizations could have... [allowed] the systematic destruction of Enron-related audit documents at a time when it was clear to everyone, certainly to Andersen, that government investigators and civil litigants would soon be demanding the documents needed to understand how things could have gone so wrong so quickly.

> *House Subcommittee investigating Enron/Andersen, January 2002*[41]

On October 16, 2001, Enron announced that it was taking a $618 million loss in its third quarter, and that it was writing down its value by more than $1 billion. Later, in December, it filed for bankruptcy—one of the largest bankruptcies in U.S. history. Months earlier, in August, the SEC had begun investigating Enron's finances, which Andersen had audited.

While Andersen itself was not being investigated at the time, it should have expected that Enron audit information it possessed would likely be of interest to investigators—especially given the size and profile of Enron's expected write down. On October 12—a day Andersen was finalizing many of Enron's audit documents in preparation for the upcoming write down announcement—Nancy Temple, one of Andersen's in-house attorneys, sent the now-infamous email message, which read:

> Mike-
> It might be useful to consider reminding the [Enron] engagement team of our documentation and retention policy. It will be helpful to make sure that we have complied with the policy. Let me know if you have any questions.
>
> > Nancy[42]

The email also provided a link to Andersen's document retention policy.

Mike Odom, a risk management partner at Andersen's Houston office, later testified that it was the first time that he had been reminded of the company's document retention policy in this manner in more than 30 years of working at Andersen.[43] Odom subsequently forwarded Temple's email message to David Duncan, the global managing partner of the Enron engagement team.[44]

During Andersen's trial, prosecutors argued that the content and timing of Temple's email "reminder" about Andersen's document retention policy suggested that it was a veiled instruction for Enron engagement team members to "clean-up" or otherwise destroy and alter Enron audit documents that would reveal incriminating information to the SEC.

According to Andersen's grand jury indictment for obstruction of justice, in a period starting just days after Temple sent the email message in October, and ending when the SEC actually issued a subpoena for Andersen's Enron documents in November,

> Andersen partners assigned to the Enron engagement team launched... a wholesale destruction of documents... Andersen personnel were called to urgent and mandatory meetings. Instead of being advised to preserve documentation so as to assist Enron and the SEC, Andersen employees on the Enron engagement team were instructed by Andersen partners and others to destroy immediately documentation relating to Enron, and told to work overtime if necessary to accomplish the destruction.
>
> During the next few weeks, an unparalleled initiative was undertaken to shred physical documentation and delete computer files. Tons of paper relating to the Enron audit were promptly shredded... A systematic effort was also undertaken and carried out to purge the computer hard-drives and email system of Enron-related files.[45]

According to the *Wall Street Journal*, Andersen later admitted that there had been an "expedited effort to dispose of Enron-related documents," but asserted that this effort had been led by David Duncan and "was undertaken without any consultation with others in the firm."[46] Andersen fired Duncan and put three other Houston partners on administrative leave. Duncan later pled guilty and testified that he had personally destroyed, and ordered the destruction of, Enron documents. He also stated that, after receiving Temple's email about the document retention policy, he had "instructed people on the [Enron audit] team to follow the document retention policy, which I knew would result in the destruction of documents."[47]

Another member of the Andersen staff in Houston testified that her boss, also a partner in Andersen's Houston office, used the phrase "follow our document retention policy" as a code meaning he wanted her to destroy documents.[48]

In March 2002, Andersen was indicted, in June it was convicted, and the following October it received the maximum penalty under the law of a $500,000 and five years of probation—largely a moot penalty as the company was all but out of business by then.

Failing to Suspend Normal Disposition Policies

Obstruction of justice is a serious crime. If you or your company gets a subpoena, don't even think about playing games with it. If you do that, you are playing with fire.

James B. Comey, U.S. attorney for the Southern District of New York[49]

The law is clear that "a party is obligated to retain evidence that it knows or reasonably should know may be relevant to pending or future litigation."[50] Furthermore, although the "service of a discovery demand places a party on notice to preserve the materials requested, the duty to preserve arises whenever a party has been served with a complaint or anticipates litigation."[51]

As the quote from the Andersen indictment above indicates, the government alleged that the company not only did not suspend the "normal" destruction of documents upon finding out about the SEC's Enron investigation, but that it in fact stepped up efforts to get rid of Enron-related documents and files.

At the first sign of the impending investigation, leadership at Andersen failed to clearly and sufficiently notify all employees that no employee should take any action whatsoever to destroy, conceal, delete, or cover up any records of its involvement with Enron. Had the managing partner clearly and repeatedly communicated the need to preserve all email, documents, work papers, and so on—even if those records could have been disposed of pursuant to company policy under normal conditions—perhaps the result could have been different.

Once litigation, audit, or investigation appears imminent, regular Information Management or Records Management rules no longer apply and must be suspended until the matter is concluded. Thereafter, anything that is even potentially relevant including drafts, duplicates, work papers, etc. that may not have needed to be retained as a company record in the first place, now have to be preserved as evidence.

According to reports, Andersen appears to have specifically instructed its employees to cease their destruction of documents only after it received the subpoena from the SEC.[52] If Andersen had disseminated and enforced a Legal Hold Policy at the first sign of trouble instead of months later when they received the subpoena, that all employees received, telling them that they had an obligation to preserve everything that might be germane to the SEC investigation, Andersen might still be in business.

Chapter 5:

Achieving IMC: Introduction to the Seven Keys

In Chapter 4 we introduced the concept of IMC, and discussed how the concepts of Compliance and Information Management fit together to provide a new approach to Information Management. Here we will introduce the Seven IMC Keys that form the basis of a methodology for all organizations to follow.

The Facts: Something Is Broken

FACT: In 2002 the Securities and Exchange Commission fines five broker-dealers a total of $8.25 million for failure to preserve email communications. In addition to the sanction, the brokerage firms are required to "review their procedures to ensure compliance with recordkeeping statutes and rules."[53]

FACT: The CEO of a public pharmaceutical company is found guilty in 2002 of obstruction of justice and other charges because he "directed another individual to... delete certain computer files... containing phone messages he received... and documents evidencing [his] instructions," although he "well knew that at the time that he directed the destruction of documents... such documents were material to the SEC's investigation" regarding insider trading.[54] The CEO is later sentenced to seven years in jail and ordered to pay a $3 million fine, the maximum penalty under the Federal Sentencing Guidelines.[55]

FACT: Fearing that yet another public company may not take its information management obligations seriously, in 2002 the SEC imposes an $800-an-hour monitor on WorldCom (now MCI). The monitor's task is to ensure that the company "has developed document retention policies and... has complied with these policies."[56]

FACT: A major federal agency notifies a flight school, six months after 9/11, that two of the 9/11 terrorists have been approved for student visas. The agency admits in 2002 that its "current system for collecting information is... antiquated, outdated, inaccurate, and untimely."[57]

FACT: The former CFO and sales manager of a defunct Internet company are indicted on charges of falsifying records and for collaborating in a scheme where the sales manager allegedly overstated revenue by $9 million (60% of revenue) in order to inflate his bonus.[58]

Allegations of records destruction, mismanagement, and falsification abound, implicating numerous companies. Billions of dollars have been erased from stock valuations, careers and reputations shattered, and companies have disappeared completely. The bankruptcy of Enron alone is estimated to have caused $70 billion in wealth to vanish.[59]

What Exactly Is Broken?

What is wrong with the way that these and other organizations are managing their information assets? Although it is difficult to narrow it down to a single set of causes in every case, there are some common elements in the failures that we have seen in the first part of this new millennium, and that continue to this day.

1. The natural result of market contraction/correction

In the boom years of the 1990s, compliance was not a high priority in all organizations. Times were good, everyone was making money, and competitive pressures to build market share and compete for a place in "the new economy" were extremely high. Many regulators couldn't keep up with the number of new companies, the new kinds of businesses activities, and the rapid pace of technology adoption.

However, as the market changes, so does the business climate. Today there is a greater focus on corporate accountability, compliance, transparency, ethics, and good governance. New accounting standards have been written and new laws have been passed. Mistakes of the boom years are now catching up with many companies as IMC activities they neglected and shortcomings they overlooked in the past are coming to light.

2. The rush to technology

Although this point is closely related to the last one, there is a separate issue that is also important. Over the past decade enterprise software and hardware spending has grown at historically unseen rates. Many new technologies have been developed, much of them centered around the ubiquity and low-cost of network connectivity offered by the Internet. As the market heated up, organizations felt even greater pressure to adopt new technologies to ensure that competitors were not gaining an advantage in their ability to meet customer expectations. In the rush to technology, "boring old" Information Management issues such as records retention often fell by the wayside. Today, the failure to confront those issues at the outset is causing problems for many organizations.

3. The design of information technology itself

In the same way that organizations in the past decade were not overly concerned about the IMC implications of new technology before implementing it, most enterprise technology was not designed with IMC in mind. Voicemail systems make it difficult to retain voicemail messages, even though they may have contractual or other legal significance. Email systems allow routine purging even though they likely contain valuable and legally significant information. Web forms and electronic documents separate content from presentation, making it difficult to capture and store a complete and accurate record. Email messages can be intercepted and altered with ease. Digital storage media have relatively short life spans and are subject to corruption. The list goes on and on.

Many vendors are responding to these needs by building in features that make it easier to capture and retain records. A recent example can be found in the ongoing maturation of Instant Messaging, which has evolved from a tool for kids, with no inherent security or retention capabilities, to an enterprise tool with a variety of configuration options for achieving IMC.

4. Authority and responsibility

Over the last two decades, as more and more company records and information were created and stored in electronic form, it became increasingly unclear exactly whose job it was to take responsibility for electronic records. What person in the organization understood archival science, Records Management, and how to configure the email system for retention? Moreover, who had the authority to design, implement, fund, and operate a program that addressed both the old world and the new world issues? The result was (and continues to be) that many IMC issues have simply fallen through the cracks.

5. Lack of a holistic view

In many organizations, governance structures and cultures have failed to evolve to account for their overwhelming reliance on electronic information. For example, the chief information officer typically sees his or her role strictly as building and maintaining the systems that house the information, and not taking responsibility for the information within those systems. The Records Management Department typically is under-funded and understaffed. Meanwhile, back-up tapes that contain email records subject to subpoena are being overwritten, with or without criminal intent.

The result is the lack of a holistic view. Such a view starts with the understanding that an organization has Information Management obligations, then seeks to understand what Information Management criteria the organization must comply with, and finally implements controls to make sure such compliance happens.

The Federal Sentencing Guidelines

As we noted in the Introduction, we used a section of the Federal Sentencing Guidelines as a model in developing the Seven Keys to IMC, which form the heart of this book. This section (Chapter 8) of the Guidelines provides seven criteria that the courts will look at when sentencing a company that is found guilty of a criminal act. Further, the Department of Justice evaluates an organization's compliance with these seven criteria "when deciding whether to prosecute corporations."[60]

Since 1991, the Federal Sentencing Guidelines have:

> Provided incentives for organizations to report violations, cooperate in criminal investigations, discipline responsible employees, and take the steps needed to prevent and detect criminal conduct by their agents. The guidelines mandate high fines for organizations that have no meaningful programs to prevent and detect criminal violations or in which management was involved in the crime. The guidelines take into account the potential range of organizational criminal culpability.
>
> *U.S. Sentencing Commission, the organization responsible for the Guidelines*[61]

Since they were published, the Guidelines have been very influential on the way that companies design and implement compliance and corporate ethics programs. They have also been adopted in various ways by a number of federal regulatory agencies, including the Department of Health and Human Services, the Environmental Protection Agency, and the Securities and Exchange Commission.[62]

The following perspectives emphasize the influence that the Guidelines have had:

> The impact of the [Federal Sentencing Guidelines] has reached well beyond the courtroom to broadly affecting corporate and organizational behavior. The Guidelines offer powerful incentives for corporations today to have in place compliance programs to detect violations of law promptly and to report violations to appropriate public officials when discovered, and

to take voluntary remedial efforts. Any rational person attempting in good faith to meet an organizational governance responsibility would be bound to take into account… the enhanced penalties and the opportunities for reduced sanction that [Federal Sentencing Guidelines] offer.

In re Caremark International Inc. Derivative Litigation[63]

The organizational guidelines have had a startling impact on the implementation of compliance and business ethics programs over the last ten years. These guidelines provide incentives for voluntary reporting and cooperation but punish an organization's failure to self-police. There is more interest than ever in these guidelines.

U.S. Sentencing Commission chair, Judge Diana E. Murphy[64]

It is easy to see why they have been so influential. Not only do the Guidelines tell companies how fines and penalties will be assessed, but they help companies determine what they can do to help avoid or reduce sanctions for wrongdoing.

Although the original focus of the Guidelines' seven criteria, or keys, is on criminal misconduct, the keys are easily adapted to the world of IMC.

In fact, not only are the seven keys adaptable, they are ideal for Information Management, and form the core of our IMC approach and methodology.

The intention in applying these Seven Keys to Information Management is not to provide an exact match between the way the keys are used in the criminal justice system and Information Management, but rather to adopt the keys for Information Management.[65]

The Seven Keys

The Seven Keys of IMC are detailed below. Part II of this book is devoted to an indepth exploration of each of these Keys.

1) **Good Policies and Procedures.** Organizations must develop and implement policies and procedures designed to

ensure that its Information Management Compliance responsibilities are addressed and its obligations are met.

2) **Executive-Level Program Responsibility.** Senior executives and managers must take overall responsibility for the Information Management Program.

3) **Proper Delegation of Program Roles and Components.** Responsibility for the Information Management programs must be delegated only to those individuals with appropriate training, qualifications, and authority.

4) **Program Communication and Training.** The organization must take steps to effectively communicate Information Management policies and procedures to all employees. These steps might include, for example, requiring all employees to participate in training programs, and the dissemination of information that explains in a practical and understandable manner what is expected of employees.

5) **Auditing and Monitoring to Measure Program Compliance.** The organization must take reasonable steps to measure compliance with Information Management policies and procedures by utilizing monitoring and auditing programs.

6) **Effective and Consistent Program Enforcement.** Information Management program policies and procedures must be consistently enforced through appropriate disciplinary mechanisms and the proper configuration and management of Information Management-related systems.

7) **Continuous Program Improvement.** When improper management of information is detected, the organization must take all reasonable steps to respond appropriately to the activity and to prevent further similar activities—including any necessary modifications to its Information Management Program.

Chapter 6:

Sarbanes-Oxley and IMC

While Sarbanes-Oxley is financial legislation, at its heart it is about ensuring that internal controls or rules are in place to govern the creation and documentation of information in financial statements. Since its systems are used to generate, change, house and transport that data, CIOs have to build the controls that ensure the information stands up to audit scrutiny.[66]

CIO Magazine, May 2003

The Sarbanes-Oxley Act of 2002 ("SOX"),[67] passed in the wake of the high-profile corporate scandals that have filled the headlines in the opening years of this decade, is a complex piece of legislation with an enormous impact on IMC. Its provisions are sweeping, and the reforms it makes to existing laws are broad. Although SOX was signed into law in 2002, its full impact is likely yet to be felt.

Organizations are spending a great deal of money and making major changes to ensure SOX compliance. A July 2003 survey showed that 91% of public company executives had made changes as a result of SOX, and indicated that a majority expected SOX compliance would cost more than they initially expected.[68] A September 2003 estimate of SOX compliance costs put the overall cost for public corporations in the billions, with an average cost per company of $500,000 in the first year alone.[69] Charges against a company and its executives under SOX have already been filed and settled.[70] A public company auditor has been arrested and charged under SOX for allegedly destroying and altering audit documents.[71] The SEC, meanwhile, filed almost 50% more "financial fraud and reporting cases" in 2002 than in the previous year.[72]

While much of the discussion around SOX has focused on its impact on corporate governance, financial reporting, and accounting practices, the law's impact extends beyond these areas. In fact, the law goes to the heart of IMC by affecting the way that organizations must manage and control information.

As a law, SOX is designed to improve the accountability and transparency of public companies. Accountability and transparency depend upon trustworthy business records because trustworthy business records are the bedrock of accounting and financial reporting systems. For example, earnings figures are derived from documentation of business transactions—purchase orders, invoices, payment information, contracts, and so on. Obviously, if any of these records are inaccurate, the information in the accounting system will be too. As a result, compliance with SOX relies on a foundation of Information Management practices designed to ensure the accuracy and trustworthiness of business records. In other words, Information Management Compliance.

This Chapter discusses the impact of SOX on IMC. It is important to note that SOX is a complex law that creates many new legal obligations. Many of these obligations have no direct bearing on Information Management and address issues specific to the public accounting profession. Furthermore, as a practical matter, SOX required the SEC to amend and add to several of its existing rules and regulations; so much of the law's impact is felt through the SEC's regulations.[73] The focus of this Chapter is limited to those sections of SOX and related regulations that affect Information Management.

Doing Business in the Post-Sarbanes-Oxley Era: Everyone Is Affected

And today I sign the most far-reaching reforms of American business practices since the time of Franklin Delano Roosevelt. This new law

*sends very clear messages that all concerned must heed. This law
says to every dishonest corporate leader: you will be exposed and
punished; the era of low standards and false profits is over; no
boardroom in America is above or beyond the law.*

U.S. President George W. Bush, signing the Sarbanes-Oxley Act,
July 30, 2002[74]

Even though SOX is aimed at public companies and their auditors, all
organizations should re-assess their approach to Information
Management in the context of SOX.[75] SOX came into being largely
because elected officials saw existing laws as insufficient to protect
the interests of the investing public, and because of a public outcry for
the government to take action to prevent and punish corporate
malfeasance. SOX was just one part of the U.S. federal government's
efforts to address these issues. The President's Corporate Fraud Task
Force, for example, was created in the same timeframe as SOX to
"aggressively investigate and prosecute fraud," and has aided in
obtaining "over 250 corporate fraud convictions or guilty pleas."[76]

Many of the high-profile cases of corporate malfeasance that ushered
in the post-SOX era (including those discussed throughout this book)
involved allegations of improper alteration and destruction of business information. As a result, issues of Information Management and
corporate fraud have become linked in the minds of corporate boards,
shareholders, and the public at large. All companies are affected by
the heightened scrutiny of internal practices that characterizes post-
SOX business era.

Furthermore, Section 802 of SOX updates the criminal code to provide stiffer criminal penalties for those who destroy information "with
the intent to impede, obstruct, or influence the investigation or proper
administration of **any matter** within the jurisdiction of any department
or agency of the United States" (emphasis added).[77] The scope of this
language suggests that SOX Section 802 criminal penalties may apply
to activities and situations that impact individuals in organizations
beyond just public companies. Section 802 is explored below.

The overall affect of SOX and related events is a greater awareness of
Information Management issues than ever before. There is a greater

realization that a consistent and effective approach to Information Management is critical to gaining and maintaining the trust of partners, customers, regulators, and even employees. Consequently, all organizations—not just public companies—need to ensure that they are responding to the new realities of this era. Many private organizations have already adopted many of the principles of SOX and used them to re-evaluate their approach to Information and Records Management. All organizations in the post-SOX era need to acknowledge the clear link between successful Information Management programs and business success as a whole.

Destruction and Alteration of Information: SOX Section 802

> *Whoever knowingly alters, destroys, mutilates, conceals, covers up, falsifies, or makes a false entry in any record, document, or tangible object with the intent to impede, obstruct, or influence the investigation or proper administration of any matter within the jurisdiction of any department or agency of the United States or any case filed under title 11, or in relation to or contemplation of any such matter or case, shall be fined under this title, **imprisoned not more than 20 years**, or both.*

Sarbanes-Oxley Section 802 (emphasis added)

Section 802 is one of the more disconcerting sections of SOX and is likely the section that initially got the attention of most organizations when SOX was signed into law. Section 802 outlines dramatic criminal penalties for the improper destruction or alteration of business records. By doing so, SOX emphasizes the reality that reliable and accurate financial reporting depends on protecting the records, documents, and other evidence that provides the foundation for that financial information.

The *disposal* of business records is as integral a part of Information Management as retention. Disposal of records according to documented policies enables organizations to get rid of information that is costly to store and manage, without fear of raising the ire of the courts or regulators. However, as explored in Chapter 4 in the context of the Andersen/Enron case, organizations also have an obligation to suspend normal disposition practices in the face of anticipated or ongoing audits, investigations, litigation, and other proceedings—including matters contemplated by Section 802.

Consequently, organizations need a mechanism (commonly referred to as a Legal or Records Hold mechanism) to inform employees of the need to preserve information. Such a mechanism should be built with the following principles in mind:

- **Decide who needs to be notified, and what they need to be told.** It is critical that the right people receive notification of the need to preserve information, and that they are provided with specific instructions on the kinds of information that must be preserved, and how it must be preserved. Notification may need to extend to contractors, outsourced storage providers, and other parties if they have responsive information (i.e., information related to the matter) in their possession, care, custody, or control.

- **All forms of information and tangible objects are included.** All recorded information regardless of the media it is stored on, and all tangible objects (such as lab samples, for example) related to the matter must be preserved.

- **Immediate action.** The obligation to suspend normal disposition practices may start the instant an organization reasonably believes that it may become involved in matters covered by Section 802. Organizations should not wait for a subpoena or other formal request for information before taking action.

- **Many kinds of "matters."** Organizations should not assume that the preservation obligation is limited to court proceedings. Section 802 provides a very broad definition of circumstances that may require special preservation activities: "**any matter** within the jurisdiction of **any department or agency** of the United States or any case filed under title 11, or **in relation to or contemplation** of any such matter or case."

- **Create and manage documentation.** Formal written policies and procedures outlining the preservation process and identifying the specific tasks and roles within the process should be created, retained, and managed as a business record. In addition, email memos, forms, and other information used to disseminate preservation notices should be retained and managed as a business record.

- **It's not just about "destruction."** Section 802 prohibits a broad range of activities beyond mere destruction, including alteration, mutilation, concealment, covering up, and falsifying. Organizations need to ensure that their Legal Hold mechanism addresses such activities. For example, purposefully disposing of proprietary software that is needed to access records during an investigation might be considered "concealment." Furthermore, allowing employees to encrypt records and "lose" the decryption key could be considered "covering up." Simply stated, the law is broader than just destruction or shredding.

Internal Controls: The Role of Information Management in Financial Reporting and Corporate Governance

The concept of "internal controls" is central to SOX, and it has a direct bearing on IMC. Section 404 of SOX requires senior management to include an "internal control report" in each annual report that assesses the effectiveness of their "internal controls and procedures... for financial reporting."[78] In addition, Section 404 requires a company's auditor to "attest to and report on" this report—in other words, to "assess the assessment." Section 302 requires CEOs and CFOs to certify in their annual and quarterly reports that they are responsible for these internal controls.[79] Section 906 provides criminal penalties including jail terms and fines of up to 20 years and $5 million, respectively, for executives who certify false financial reports.[80]

Although the concept of "internal controls" as used in SOX is well-known in the public accounting world, it is less well-known in the Information Management world. However, in the post-SOX era, individuals with responsibility for Information Management in all organizations needs to become familiar with this key SOX concept.

Internal Controls

The term 'internal control' over financial reporting is defined as a process designed by, or under the supervision of [the company's senior executives] and effected by the [company's] board of directors, management and other personnel, to provide reasonable assurance **regarding the reliability of financial reporting** and the preparation of financial statements for external purposes in accordance with generally accepted accounting principles and includes those policies and procedures that:

1. **Pertain to the maintenance of records that in reasonable detail accurately and fairly reflect the transactions** and dispositions of the assets of the issuer;

2. **Provide reasonable assurance that transactions are recorded as necessary to permit preparation of financial statements** in accordance with generally accepted accounting principles, and that receipts and expenditures of the issuer are being made only in accordance with authorizations of management and directors of the issuer; and

3. Provide reasonable assurance regarding prevention or timely detection of unauthorized acquisition, use or disposition of the issuer's assets that could have a material effect on the financial statements.

Exchange Act 13a-15(f) (emphasis added in bold throughout)

This definition, which comes from a key SEC regulation implementing SOX,[81] makes clear that "internal controls" have a scope that extends to Information Management practices. As stated by the definition, internal controls include "policies and procedures" designed to ensure that critical records are managed in such as way that they "accurately and fairly reflect" an organization's business transactions." Further, these policies and procedures should "provide reasonable assurance that transactions are recorded as necessary" to support accurate financial reporting and good corporate governance. These goals and concepts should sound familiar to anyone with experience in designing and implement Information and Records Management programs.

Although the concept of internal controls clearly encompasses the specialized tools and techniques employed in public accounting and financial reporting, it seems clear that Information Management policies, techniques, and programs are also a key form of internal control that organizations need to employ in order to have confidence in the statements made in their Section 404 "internal control report," statements and Section 302 certifications. Information Management programs are, after all, explicitly designed to ensure the trustworthiness and accuracy of records that document business activities and transactions.

Information Management and SOX

In the post-SOX era, organizations must ensure that their approach to Information Management is one that supports the organization's need for trustworthy and accurate financial information. Information Management programs must give executives comfort that the information they are certifying to comply with SOX is trustworthy, accurate, and can be supported by the organization's own business records.

Information Management programs provide critical "internal controls" that are central to ensuring that an organization can meet SOX requirements for the reliability and accuracy of financial reporting. The integrity and accessibility of records and other business information must be protected at all times—a requirement that takes on even greater importance when an organization anticipates or is involved in audits, investigations, litigation, or other formal proceedings. Organizations need to have a mechanism for ensuring that the right people throughout the organization are informed of the need to preserve responsive information.

Information Management Preparedness Checklist

Here are some activities (not all by any means) that you might undertake to achieve IMC in your organization:

1) Educate employees regarding the ownership of company information—for example, who "owns" the information that a salesperson enters on his or her laptop and handheld computers?

2) Provide employees with rules for the secure transmission of electronic information.

3) Develop a privacy policy for the organization's website, another privacy policy for employees' personal information that resides in human resources records, and a third privacy policy, if applicable, for personal information about individual customers, clients, or patients.

4) Use Document Management and Records Management software and require all employees who use that software to be trained regarding its proper use.

5) Provide employees (especially IT staff) with written procedures for properly scanning, imaging, indexing, and storing records from paper to optical disc.

6) Create, disseminate, monitor, and enforce compliance with an Information Management policy.

7) Give certain employees in each business unit responsibility for Records Management as part of their job description.

PART 2

Seven Keys to Information Management Compliance

Key #1

Good Policies and Procedures

Organizations must develop and implement policies and procedures designed to ensure that its Information Management Compliance responsibilities are addressed and its obligations are met.

Key Overview

Policies and procedures provide the foundation of every Information Management program. Policies are a manifestation of an organization's beliefs about Information Management, and they express an organization's commitment to sound management—an important message not only to employees but to the outside world as well.

The Overview

Chapter 7:

The Purpose of Policies and Procedures

Laying the Foundation of IMC

> *The company has "no comprehensive document retention policy with informative guidelines and lacks a protocol that promptly notifies senior management of document destruction. These systemic failures impede the litigation process and merit the imposition of sanctions."*
>
> *In re Prudential Ins. Co. of America Sales Practices Litigation*[82]

In the case mentioned above, the company failed to create adequate policies for the preservation of evidence related to litigation, and as a result (at least in part), paid a $1 million fine. There have been countless other cases where organizations paid a price simply because they did not invest the time and money required to create a set of policies and procedures adequate to address their Information Management needs. Policies and procedures don't need to be complex—in fact, often the simpler they are, the better.

Policies and procedures are the management tools that an organizations uses to codify and communicate its approach to Information Management. They serve a variety of legal, compliance, operational, and business purposes. And, in the context of IMC, they provide the *criteria* that the *program* itself must *comply with*.

The Difference between Policies and Procedures

Policies and procedures work together to provide a two-tiered set of directives and guidelines. While policies provide a high-level articulation of an organization's position on particular issues, procedures bring those positions down to earth by laying out specific actions and responsibilities.

Information Management policies, without procedures, may not provide sufficient detail and direction to work effectively as guidance to employees. For example, an Information Management policy may contain a statement like this:

> Our company must retain evidence of our business transactions in order to comply with laws, regulations, and our business and operational requirements.

A nice statement, but one that may be of little value or meaning to an employee trying to determine whether or not he or she should retain a particular email message, voicemail message, or Instant Message.

Or what about the technologist trying to determine how to build an online application that allows customers to sign up for new services on the company's website? How should he or she build the application so that it captures and preserves information required by law, or to meet the company's operational requirements? Companies often face this issue when building Web-based applications.

Questions like these can only be answered through clear and detailed procedures that implement the policy. Policies and practices may exist in separate documents, but not necessarily. For example, a Records Management manual often contains a combination of policy statements (such as the Records Management program's purpose) and specific directives (such as step-by-step instructions for retaining specific kinds of records).

Provide Clear Directives to Employees

Without clearly written and widely disseminated policies and procedures, how can an organization expect its employees to know what their Information Management obligations are? It cannot, especially in larger organizations where consistency is an even larger challenge.

Good policies and procedures should:

- Provide insight to employees on what management believes is important, thereby helping to establish the organization's culture and to set employee and management expectations.

- Clarify in plain language what each employee's Information Management obligations are, why the obligations exist, and what will happen if the employee fails to follow the directives.

- Provide consistent guidelines for employee behavior that last beyond the residency of a particular manager or executive. In this sense, policies and procedures are part of the soul of an organization—they continue to live on long past their authors, and provide a compass for ongoing organizational behavior.

Making a Statement to the World

Written policies and procedures make a statement to the outside world that an organization cares strongly about an issue. Widely disseminating policies and training employees on its implementation serves to emphasize an organization's commitment to addressing Information Management issues.

Making this statement to the outside world is not just a public relations strategy. In fact, it can be an important mitigating factor when mistakes do happen. If an organization can demonstrate to an investigator, regulator, court, or even the media that they had a policy in place and trained employees to follow the policy, then isolated failures are much more likely to be seen as individual accidents rather than organizational failures.

In the Prudential case quoted at the beginning of this chapter, the court was seemingly angry not because employees destroyed relevant evidence, but rather because the company failed to have policies and procedures in place that would have helped to prevent the destruction. The judge stated, in part:

> While there is no proof that Prudential, through its employees, engaged in conduct intended to thwart discovery through the purposeful destruction of documents, its haphazard and uncoordinated approach to document retention indisputably denies its party opponents potential evidence to establish facts in dispute.[83]

Would the judge have fined Prudential $1 million if the company's policies and procedures had demonstrated that it took reasonable steps to ensure that it would consistently meet its Information Management obligations? Not as likely.

Not Following Your Own Policy Is Bad Policy

There are many cases in which having the right policies and procedures but not following them is as bad or perhaps worse than not having policies or procedures in the first place. This is clearly demonstrated in *Kentucky Cent. Life Ins. Co. v. Jones*,[84] where a dispute over the accuracy of the defendant's medical records resulted from failing to follow a hospital policy.

The hospital where the defendant was a patient had a policy that required the admitting doctor to dictate the patient's case history within 48 hours. However, the doctor in this case failed to follow the policy, only providing the information five weeks later. This delay created an opportunity for the argument that the medical records were not trustworthy and accurate, and as such should not be admitted in evidence.

The very existence of the dictation policy suggests that the hospital itself believed that adherence to the policy was necessary to prevent lapses in the doctor's memory from reducing the accuracy of patient records. If this was the hospital's logic, as borne out by the policy, then why should they not be held accountable to that logic in the context of a dispute?

Furthermore, while the intent of the policy seems sound, it also seems that there was not an adequate system in place to ensure that the policy was followed. Aside from the potential risk to patients, this failure resulted in longer and more expensive litigation, as the parties had to address the veracity of the records at issue.

If You Don't Do It, Someone Else Will

SEC, NYSE, NASD Fine Five Firms Total of $8.25 Million for Failure to Preserve Email Communications

The Securities and Exchange Commission, the New York Stock Exchange and NASD today announced joint actions against five broker-dealers for violations of record-keeping requirements regarding e-mail communications. The firms consented to the imposition of fines totaling $8.25 million, along with a requirement to review their procedures to ensure compliance with record-keeping statutes and rules.[85]

In 2002, five large Wall Street firms were fined $8.25 million for failing to properly preserve and manage email communications pertaining to their business. The SEC ordered each company to review their email management procedures and to prove within 90 days "it has established systems and procedures reasonably designed to achieve compliance with the statute and rules relating to email retention."

When the SEC fined these firms, it provided detailed information on its areas of concern. Examine your own Information Management policies, procedures, and practices against these all-too-common issues.

- **No procedures and controls.** "Each firm had inadequate procedures and systems to retain and make accessible email communications."

- **No management guidance or system provision.** "While some firms relied on employees to preserve copies of the email communications on the hard drives of their individual personal computers, there were no systems or procedures to ensure that employees did so."

- **Back-up is not retention.** Some firms said that they were backing up email for disaster recovery or business continuity purposes, but "these firms discarded or recycled and over-wrote their back-up tapes and other media, often a year or less after back-up occurred." (Note that the SEC requires broker's email "communications" to be retained for a minimum of three years.)

- **Lack of uniform procedures.** When the firms did retain email, the email was "often stored in an unorganized fashion on back-up tapes, other media, or on the hard drives of computers used by individual employees."

- **Departing employees.** "In some instances, hard drives of computers preserving electronic mail communications were erased when individuals left the employment of the firm."

While the fines in this case were not inconsequential, the more damaging and costly result in the long run may be the fact that regulators are now poised to watch the firms' every move.

Putting It Down in Writing

Policies and procedures are formal, written documents that are carefully managed and disseminated to ensure that their contents stay up-to-date and accurate. There is a reason for this formality.

Policies and procedures serve to formally document and provide proof of an organization's commitment and practices at a particular time, should there be a dispute in the future about its intent. The need for this formality may be less in smaller organizations, where the daily contact between supervisors and employees may allow company directives to be disseminated more informally.

The courts have recognized this distinction between large and small companies. For example, in *Faragher v. City of Boca Raton*,[86] the court acknowledged that "the employer of a small workforce" might expect that its duty to exercise "sufficient care" to provide a safe workplace "could be exercised informally," whereas an employer with many departments and "far-flung" employees would require a "formal policy."

There are two primary ways that an organization "speaks" in the course of investigations and litigation: through its employees and through its business records. Policies and procedures not only provide standards for how employees should behave when acting on the organization's behalf, they tell a story about the organization's priorities, commitment, and actions, which is important in the legal context.

A Case for Formality

A pharmaceutical company's IT department creates a new workflow application that is designed to make the process of new drug applications much faster and more efficient by eliminating paper. Instead of using handwritten signatures, system users are given user ID and passwords that they can type into the system to affix an "electronic signature" on a digital document.

The employees are given a quick briefing on how to use the system, which includes a warning (not in writing) that their electronic signatures are for their use only and are not to be shared with other employees.

A few weeks later, working under a tight deadline, an employee named Theodore tries to access the system. After trying to enter his password three or four times, he realizes that he forgot his password, and shouts over the cubicle to Dylan to get his user ID and password. Theodore then uses Dylan's password to access and digitally sign an important application for FDA approval.

The next month, during an FDA investigation, a question arises about that particular application. The FDA wants to know who signed the document. The log files show that Dylan signed the document, but he claims that he knows nothing about it. He then remembers that Theodore "borrowed" his password one day. Questions about the identity of the signer call the entire electronic signature system into question, the FDA investigation intensifies, and sanctions are assessed. Dylan is fired for sharing his password in violation of company policy.

Dylan then sues the company for wrongful termination. In the ensuing litigation, the company can provide no convincing evidence that it ever had a policy forbidding the sharing of user IDs and passwords. Dylan wins his case, and the company pays—a double whammy that could have been easily prevented by putting into writing, and preserving, the oral admonition that the company gave to employees during training for the new system.

For more information about password policies, see page 231.

Limiting Corporate Liability for Employee Actions

One of the primary goals of compliant Information Management policies and procedures is to help organizations avoid liability for their employees' actions.

As discussed in Chapter 4 and throughout the book, a key element of the Andersen/Enron case was the issue of employer liability for an employee's actions. Even though Andersen did have a policy regarding document destruction in place, the company was still found liable for the actions of its employees, and was not "shielded" from liability, probably due in part because they failed to enforce their policy. Notwithstanding the outcome of this case, which was likely influenced by the massive scale of the alleged fraud, the courts have recognized that organizations may be able to limit the liability caused by the "bad acts" of their employers.

Scenario 1: Pornography Sent Through Instant Messaging

Consider a fictional (but all too real) scenario where a female employee receives a pornographic image from a male employee through the company's Instant Messaging system, and files a harassment complaint. The company has an "electronic communications policy" that stipulates "the company's IM system cannot be used to send, receive, or display pornographic or violent images." The company also provides procedures in the employee manual for filing a complaint about any violation of company policy. The human resources department responds to the complaint by firing the employee who sent the offensive image.

In the ensuing wrongful termination dispute, the existence of the policy and the complaint procedure is likely to mitigate the liability attached to the company for the act of "harassment" by the employee who contravened the policy. While the company may not completely escape sanctions for the harassment, the damages will likely be much less that they otherwise would be.

Scenario 2: The Unencrypted Email

In this fictional scenario, a hospital creates a new policy to respond to the new requirements of the Health Insurance Portability and Accountability Act (HIPAA). Among other things, the new policy requires "that any email containing personal identifiable information be encrypted when sent outside the company firewall."

An employee accidentally misaddresses an unencrypted email message intended for Patient A, and it ends up in Patient B's inbox, unencrypted. Patient A is outraged and files a complaint, claiming that the hospital has violated the privacy of medical information in its possession.

During the ensuing dispute, the hospital provides a copy of the policy requiring encryption. It cannot, however, provide any convincing evidence that it ever trained employees how to use the encryption features of its email software, or even ensure that each employee had access to the appropriate encryption software.

In this case, although the existence of a policy may provide some mitigation of liability, the company's failure to follow through with policy implementation, procedures, and training will not work in its favor. It will be harder for the company to argue that the release of private records to the wrong person was simply a mistake on the part of a single employee.

Chapter 8:

Making Good Policies and Procedures

In the last chapter we looked at the need for Information Management policies and procedures. In this chapter we will look at strategies that organizations can use to make good policies and procedures that address their IMC needs.

Create a Policy and Procedure Structure

In smaller organizations, a single policy document may be enough to address most Information Management issues. However, most medium- and large-sized organizations will require a number of different policy and procedure documents to adequately address the Information Management needs of different departments and different operations.

As such, organizations need to make sure that they not only have the right policies and procedures, but also that these various documents work together as "seamlessly" as possible. This can be challenging in complex environments where there are many departments with diverse needs.

Each organization will take a different approach to Information Management policies and procedures, based on a number of factors, including the nature of its business, its organizational culture, and its regulatory environment. In other words, there is no standard, one-size-fits-all policy.

Records Management Policies and Procedures

There are several ways to structure the policies and procedures of a Records Management program, but there are also many consistent elements. For example, they should start with broad, high-level policies that govern the entire organization. Here are some examples of high-level policy tools.

1) **High-Level Information Management and Records Management Policy Manual.** This policy provides high-level, principle-based guidance for the entire organization, and provides the minimum standards that must be followed by all departments and groups. It is the foundation of all other policies and procedures created or adopted throughout the organization. Thus, it needs to be broad enough to accommodate different needs, yet specific enough to provide useful guidance.

2) **Organizational Retention Rules.** A detailed document that provides retention periods for different categories of records in the organization, and indicates the legal, regulatory, or business reasons for each retention period.

3) **Electronic Records Policy.** Although it may be appropriate to address specific electronic records issues in the general Records Management policy, it may also be necessary to create a separate policy to address specific electronic records issues. A separate document can be useful in terms of bringing specific focus to electronic records issues, and addressing issues that may be generally new or unfamiliar to employees.

4) **Records Hold Policy.** As explored in Chapter 4 (discussing the Andersen/Enron case), organizations need a mechanism for informing affected individuals and departments when normal Information Management practices must be suspended due to anticipated or commenced investigations, audits, or litigation. The Records Hold policy and related procedures also may provide forms and other standard documents to be used for the legal, compliance, tax, and/or audit departments to disseminate information on the occasion of a Records Hold.

Create Clear and Unambiguous Directives

Policies and practices do little good if employees cannot understand them, or if the directives are unclear or ambiguous. Particularly where information technology use is being addressed, many organizations seem tempted to use vague language that doesn't require them to investigate all the implications of a policy on the end-user or administrator.

Avoid Technology Snafus

The need for clarity is illustrated in the hypothetical case of a medical insurer whose policy states:

> All business areas may use electronic technologies to manage and store their business content, provided it is done properly and adequately.

Based on that policy "guidance" from the head office, a regional office moves ahead with plans to purchase and install a large imaging system to convert all existing paper records to electronic form. To save time and bring the project in under budget, they decide that initially, the only "metadata" (data about data) that will be entered about each record in the database for indexing and search purposes is the claim number.

Years and millions of images later, the company is sued by a group of customers, and in the course of the litigation, all documents related to those customers are requested. However, because the company could not search the imaged records by any criteria other than claim number, they are forced to spend tens of thousands of dollars and hundreds of hours manually searching through their database of imaged records to find those responsive to the discovery order.

The company's failure to provide detailed directives on proper indexing of electronic imaged records exposed the company to unnecessary expense. Had the company's imaging experts been consulted by the policy makers, they might have explained how they developed their imaging procedures, which took into consideration such laws as IRS Revenue Procedure Ruling 97-22, which requires "an indexing system for records retrieval" (see page 209 for more information about this IRS rule and its impact on IMC).

Personal Use of Company Resources

A company has a policy that states:

> Employees may use company computer resources for personal reasons to the extent such use does not waste company resources, impair system functionality, or impair job performance.

Mel Brick, a new accountant at the company, decides to download music from his favorite bands using a P2P file sharing program. Having just read the employee manual after he was hired, the company's policy is fresh in his mind, so he is careful to download music only during his lunch break.

Days later, a certified letter from a record industry lawyer arrives, informing the company that it is being sued for infringing on nearly a dozen musicians' intellectual property rights. The company's information security guru seizes Mr. Brick's computer and finds the infringing songs, as well as three pornographic movies that Brick claims he did not download. Also, it becomes clear that Mel has inadvertently provided access to all the files on his computer, including confidential financial information, by tapping into the file sharing network.

Here is clear case of a company failing to provide clear and sufficiently detailed guidance to its employees. Mel Brick thought he was properly interpreting the vague language found in the policy and, coupled with some technological ignorance, he has put the company in jeopardy. Not only is the policy unclear on what activities are permissible, but also it gives no clue as to what is considered a waste of company resources.

Although it is not possible or practical to anticipate all the specific ways that employees may use "company computer resources for personal reasons," organizations do have a responsibility to anticipate the Information Management implications of the technology they provide to employees. In this example, the company should have been aware of the legal and security implications of P2P file sharing over the Internet, and specifically have prohibited employees from using this technology through policy.

See page 110 for more information about addressing personal use of organizational resources at work.

Keys to Clarity

Organizations are sometimes under the illusion that broad, vague, or general language will make their policies and procedures more flexible, or give them latitude in the way they enforce them.

However, clear, precise, and unambiguous language protects the organization by limiting interpretation, thus providing greater certainty about the outcome of a dispute. It also minimizes the likelihood of violations in the first place.

In cases where there is ambiguity in the language of a policy and procedure, the courts typically interpret the document in a way that favors the employee, not the employer that drafted the language.

Techniques that organizations can use in drafting clear, unambiguous policies:

- Use examples and illustrations.

- Be brief and concise. Sometimes the more you try to explain, the more confusing it becomes.

- Separate individual policies and procedures into discrete documents when possible, instead of providing one long, run-on manual that employees are less likely to read through because of the overwhelming length.

- Require employees to sign and "certify" that they have received, read, and understood the policies and procedures given to them. At a minimum, repeat the process whenever major policy changes are made.

Policies in the Real World

When policies and procedures are put to the test in the real world, you can be sure that any weakness in their development, implementation, and enforcement will be exposed and possibly used against you. The case of *Palmer v. Lenfest Group*[87] clearly illustrates this point.

Lenfest, a local cable company, provided free basic and premium cable service to its employees as a job perk. But employees were required to pay 50% for some other services, such as pay-per-view. Some employees who handled customer accounts also had the ability to access their own accounts, but company policy prohibited them from doing so.

The policy prohibiting employees from making changes to their own accounts and related documentation was not included in the employee manual, but instead was emailed to company managers to be distributed to the employees who reported to them. In addition, the requirement to pay 50% of pay-per-view services was not in the employee manual or in any written policy, perhaps because the manual and policies had not been updated since the company had introduced pay-per-view technology.

According to the court, Palmer, a dispatcher at Lenfest, failed to pay her $68 cable bill, and her cable service was scheduled for disconnection. Palmer accessed her own account and gave herself a payment extension. When that deadline passed, her cable was automatically disconnected. She once again accessed the system and reversed the disconnection.

When Palmer's unauthorized changes were finally discovered, Palmer was terminated for theft of company property (cable TV services), and a legal dispute over unemployment benefits ensued. Even though the company eventually won the case, a nasty and expensive legal battle that dragged on for months likely could have been avoided if the company had been more vigilant in the way that it implemented and enforced its policies and procedures.

What We Can Learn

- **Keep policies up-to-date.** Policies need to be regularly reviewed and updated. The cable company failed to update its policies to keep pace with technology, which allowed Palmer to argue that she did not have to pay her 50% share for pay-per-view services. In addition, the employee manual did not explicitly state that updates to the manual could be distributed via email, which raised doubt about the legitimacy of the policy sent via email in this case.

- **Don't over-rely on policies.** The case likely would never have happened if employees were not given access to their own accounts. In most technology environments, it would be easy for administrators to use IDs and passwords to restrict access only to authorized employees.

- **Monitor compliance.** Since Palmer accessed her account more than once in violation of policy, a system of compliance monitoring might have detected the violation earlier.

- **Be consistent.** Palmer defended her access and changing of her account by stating: "I've done it before without any ramification and that's why I did not believe there would be any ramifications this time." Employers must consistently follow their own policies in order for them to have value.

- **Email must be used carefully for policy notices.** Unlike the paper-based employee manual, which Palmer had signed, there was no easy way to demonstrate that the employee had received, read, and understood the policy sent to her via email. The employer did provide email records that showed that the email had been sent to Palmer, but doubt in this area was a central part of the dispute. There are better digital methods that can be used to show that an employee accessed and even electronically signed a policy. Many companies use their intranet for this purpose, for example. In addition, the decision to send the email first to supervisors, who then had responsibility to send it on to their reports, was not a best practice, as it contributed to creating doubt about whether or not Palmer received the email message containing the policy.

Policies Should Be Technology-Neutral

Information Management policies that address information technology should be "technology-neutral." That is, they should be written in such a way that they would not go out of date when an organization's technology practices change or when new technology is adopted. The vast majority of laws that address information technology take the same approach: by covering broad principles and goals they can stand the test of time while the technology landscape shifts around them.

This is also one of the reasons why statutes are generally broad, whereas the regulations that implement the statutes are more specific, and often do provide specific technical and procedural requirements. In much the same way, it will often be necessary to provide employees with directives and instructions that specifically address the right way to use a particular technology—guidance that will have to be kept up-to-date if the technology implementation changes. Such directives and instructions support the broader policy. This guidance often takes the form of training materials.

Making company-wide policy is often a laborious and expensive task, so it is a good practice to write policies that remain relevant for the longest period possible. That being said, organizations also have to build a process for periodic review and revision of policies, to accommodate changes in the law, business focus and structure, technology, and so on.

For example, consider the following policy directive:

> All confidential information must be encrypted before being transmitted over the Internet.

This statement is technology-neutral in two ways. First, it does not specify the technology used to transmit the information over the Internet, so it is "neutral" enough to encompass email, Instant Messaging, or other digital communications technologies that the company may use now or in the future. Second, it does not stipulate the method of encryption that must be used, which allows the company to employ the best methods and products available at any time.

On the other hand, consider this policy statement:

> Employees must use the encryption feature of their email program to encrypt all email messages transmitted over the Internet.

This statement would need to be complemented by other policy and/or procedural statements addressing additional digital communication tools. Also, it would need to be updated if the company changed the method or software program used for encrypting email.

Writing technology-neutral policy statements in the first place can give policies more longevity.

Guiding IT/IS with Policies and Procedures

Your organization's IT/IS department needs to be guided by Information Management policies and procedures when selecting, building, configuring, and maintaining technology. Each choice made by IT staff in these areas can have a major impact on your organization's ability to meet its Information Management goals and obligations.

For example, in 1997, the FDA released 21 CFR Part 11, a regulation that allows the use of electronic records and signatures in the pharmaceutical industry. The purpose of Part 11 was to "permit the widest possible use of electronic technology, compatible with FDA's responsibility to protect the public health."[88]

Part 11 provides detailed requirements for compliant information systems. The impact of these requirements on the selection, creation, configuration, and management of IT systems in the industry is wide-ranging and complex. In fact, the FDA has since released guidance on several occasions specifically designed to help companies understand the implications of the regulation on these activities.[89]

Some of the requirements of Part 11 for compliant IT systems include:

- System validation
- Electronic copies
- Records protection
- System access
- Secure, computer-generated, time stamped audit trails
- Operational sequencing checks
- Authority checks

- Device checks

- Written policies for signature users

- Documentation controls

The policies and procedures that inform the selection, building, and management of IT systems that comply with these requirements requires a great deal of collaboration amongst technology, legal, compliance, and other areas of an organization—with the key principle being that the policies drive the technology, and not the other way around.

Organizations also face the choice of buying or building systems that are compliant. As mentioned on page 36, some technology vendors produce "off-the-shelf" software and hardware that is specifically designed to address a variety of compliance needs, such as the storage and management of electronic records in compliance with industry electronic records regulations such as FDA Part 11, SEC Rule 17a-4, and a variety of related laws and regulations. Many of these products are also designed to integrate with and complement internal solutions that are custom-built to address organizations' unique operating needs.

Resist the Temptation to Make Catch-All Policies

The electronic age has been a boon to the policy drafters. Companies not only need email policies, they also need email etiquette guidelines, email record retention rules, Instant Messaging policies, Internet "appropriate use" guidelines, and so on. While there may be lots of policies to draft, when you take on the task of drafting a policy related to Information Management, make sure the scope is clearly defined and that you do not take on too much.

It may be tempting to create the "everything, including the kitchen sink" policy that is designed to cover all your Information Management issues in one shot, but such efforts are usually doomed to failure. Success is much more likely if you start out with a few of the key issues that need to be addressed, cover them in smaller policies, then move on and add to your body of policy over time. Successive policies can be consolidated and revised down the road if needed.

That being said, it is also important to consult with stakeholders, and sketch out a short-, medium-, and long-term drafting roadmap, taking into consideration high-level policy imperatives before any drafting begins. This will ensure that the overall scope of your Information Management program is broad enough, and there is not a great deal of confusing overlap amongst the various policies that are created along the way.

Address Ongoing Changes in the Law

From time to time, there will be changes in laws and regulations that will require you to change Information Management policies and procedures. For example, consider the case of a multinational company that has an email policy that states:

> Employees have no right to privacy with respect to email on the company email system, and the company may review, access, or monitor email usage and message content.

The company has a division in France, where the Social Chamber of the Supreme Court ruled in 2001 that employee email could not be accessed and viewed by an employer, even if the company advised employees that it would do so. On the heels of that ruling, company policy clearly needs to change to reflect the change in law.

However, if the policy had been written as follows, no change would be required and the policy would still work universally throughout the entire organizations:

> The company reserves the right to review, access, monitor, audit, or make available any email messages on the company email system, to the full extent allowed by law.

Other recent legal changes brought about by new or updated laws and regulations, such as Sarbanes-Oxley, have also required many companies to revisit Information Management policies and procedures. For example, Sarbanes-Oxley lengthens the time that public company auditors need to keep audit work papers—a change that may need to be reflected in up-to-date retention rules.

Addressing Policy Violations: A Four-Stage Program Courtesy of the FTC

Sometimes it's the simplest things that get you in trouble. How many people have typed an email address in the "to" or "cc" box of their email program that they actually meant to put in the "bcc" box—thereby revealing to the recipients exactly who else is getting the same message? For most people, the consequences of this little slip up are probably minimal—maybe a little embarrassment.

However, when one of the world's largest drug makers makes a similar mistake, it's a different story. In 2002, an FTC investigation revealed that a major pharmaceutical company had sent an email message to nearly 700 Prozac users that unintentionally included each user's email address in plain sight in the email message's "to" field. In other words, 700 people just found out that you use Prozac.

Not only was this embarrassing for the company, but it also violated the trust of its customers, not to mention its own privacy policy.

According to the FTC, the company "failed to maintain or implement internal measures appropriate under the circumstances to protect sensitive consumer information."

In fact, the FTC said that the company failed to:

1) "provide appropriate training for its employees;"

2) "provide appropriate oversight and assistance for the employee who sent out the email, who had no prior experience in creating, testing, or implementing the computer program used;" and,

3) "implement appropriate checks and controls on the process."

The FTC also stated that the company also "violated a number of its own written security procedures."

Under the FTC settlement that resulted, the company was required to "establish and maintain a four-stage information security program," which required the company to:

1) designate appropriate personnel to coordinate and oversee the program;

2) identify reasonably foreseeable internal and external risks to the security, confidentiality, and integrity of personal information, including any such risks posed by lack of training, and to address these risks in each relevant area of its operations, whether performed by employees or agents, including: (i) management and training of personnel; (ii) information systems for the processing, storage, transmission, or disposal of personal information; and (iii) prevention and response to attacks, intrusions, unauthorized access, or other information systems failures;

3) conduct an annual written review by qualified persons, within ninety (90) days after the date of service of the order and yearly thereafter, which shall monitor and document compliance with the program, evaluate the program's effectiveness, and recommend changes to it; and,

4) adjust the program in light of any findings and recommendations resulting from reviews or ongoing monitoring, and in light of any material changes to [the company's] operations that affect the program.[90]

The FTC's analysis of the problem in this case is instructive. Although it is clearly impossible to prevent employees from making mistakes entirely, it is possible to design and implement Information Management programs that minimize the likelihood of such mistakes occurring—and minimize the magnitude of such mistakes when they do occur. The program outlined by the FTC here also introduces auditing and monitoring principles that will be explored in greater detail in Key 5.

Chapter 9:

Information Management Policy Issues

A compliant Information Management program must address myriad policy issues. The intention of this chapter is not, however, to provide a catalogue of those issues. Rather, this chapter focuses on a selection of issues that are worthy of specific focus because they commonly seem to cause problems for organizations, either because of their complexity or their relative newness.

Issue #1: The Technology/Policy Cycle

Information technology is clearly transforming business today. A recent survey conducted by AIIM International and Kahn Consulting, Inc., found—no surprise here—that fully 100% of organizations surveyed use email to conduct business.[91] Also as expected, nearly every organization uses laptop computers and voicemail (both 98%), but organizations are also using a surprising variety of less common technologies—including Instant Messaging, message boards, and peer-to-peer (P2P) file sharing for business purposes.

However, while most organizations surveyed allow employees to use these technologies, many fail to ensure that they have adequate policies in place. For example, even though 59% of organizations allow employees to use newsgroups for business, only 17% of organizations provide formal, written policies for their use. It's much the same story with wireless-enabled handheld devices such as personal digital assistants and tablet PCs, where 81% of organizations allow their use but only 28% have formal, written policies.

P2P file sharing is no better, with less than half of organizations that allow its use providing employees with written guidelines, despite recent cases where companies have become embroiled in copyright disputes over music files shared over the corporate network. Instant Messaging is graduating from a chat tool for teenagers to an enterprise messaging tool with real business uses and real legal implications. Forty-six percent of organizations use it for business, but less than half of those have a formal policy—this despite new rules from regulators like the National Association of Securities Dealers that require Instant Messaging communications to be retained by brokerage companies like any other business correspondence.

The disconnect between the use of these technologies and the lack of rules to control their use is problematic. Failure to provide rules creates security risks and retention issues, and may allow technology to be used in a way that does not promote business interests.

Some of this policy vacuum can be attributed to the lag time that naturally occurs between a technology's adoption and the creation of a policy. In other cases, the cause is not so clear. For example, the fact that text messaging or email-enabled mobile phones are relatively new to many organizations may partly explain why only 21% of organizations have written policies even though a majority of them (59%) allow their use. However, it is hard to apply the same logic to newsgroups (59% use/17% policies) or file transfer protocol (82% use/35% policy), since both are mature technologies that have been in widespread use for decades. In many organizations, the reason for this neglect may be simply (yet potentially dangerous) that they have never had a problem with the technology, so they haven't felt a need to control its use.

A passive approach to policy making can be dangerous, as the business world learned over the past decade or so, especially as email evolved to become the commonplace tool it is today. In the nascent days of email use, organizations took a passive approach to email management. This passiveness forced them to react to expensive mistakes, violations, and problems after the fact by drafting policies, training, auditing, monitoring, retraining, and occasionally firing violators—just to get email use under control. Offering businesses an incredible boost in efficiency, email was rolled out across the business world, with tremendous enthusiasm, without a great deal of consideration of the potential liability that lay within the email system. As you might expect, much that could go wrong did go wrong. Consequently organizations were forced to reduce risk and improve performance through policy or other means. Now, while some employees still violate email policies (and a few employees likely always will) the majority of organizations (80%) have "prohibited use" policies, at a minimum, that tell the workforce how to deal with all kinds of conduct that could get the employees and the organization in serious trouble.

Issue #2: Electronic Discovery

> In this... era of widely publicized evidence destruction by document shredding, it is well to remind litigants that such conduct will not be tolerated in judicial proceedings. Destruction of evidence cannot be countenanced in a justice system whose goal is to find the truth through honest and orderly production of evidence under established discovery rules.
>
> Cabnetware, Inc. v. Sullivan[92]

Increased reliance on information technology has inevitably led to greater use of electronic evidence in litigation, investigations, audits, and other formal proceedings. In fact, according to the courts, "[c]omputers have become so commonplace that most court battles now involve discovery of some type of computer-stored information."[93] Litigators often take advantage of this lack of preparation by making digital information, especially email, a target of discovery.

Every organization involved in litigation, audits, investigations, and other formal proceedings need to turn over all relevant information in their "care, custody, or control" to the opposing side (unless subject to a privilege, such as attorney-client), regardless of how embarrassing or damaging it is. Additionally, regulators and auditors may ask for information regarding transactions that occurred years earlier.

What Is Discoverable?

All parties in litigation must disclose "a copy of, or a description by category and location of, all documents, data compilations, and tangible things that are in the possession, custody, or control of the party and that the disclosing party may use to support its claims or defenses…"

Federal Rules of Civil Procedure[94]

The Federal Rules of Civil Procedure, which provide discovery rules (among other things) for federal courts, define a discoverable "document" as including, "writings, drawings, graphs, charts, photographs, phonorecords, and other data compilations from which information can be obtained, translated, if necessary, by the respondent through detection devices into reasonably usable form."[95] As this definition of discoverable information is very broad, it could be applied to nearly any type of electronic information imaginable.

Because of the scope of allowable electronic discovery, organizations need to think beyond traditional definitions of an "electronic record" or "document," and consider the entire range of digital information that may be subject to a discovery order. While the need to produce word processing and spreadsheet documents may be obvious to most organizations, email, Instant Messages, presentations, server log files, HTML code, and other "casual" or "hidden" types of evidence may not be.

An organization's electronic discovery plan should consider the full range of electronic information that the courts may require it to find and produce.

What Secrets Are Lurking on Your Computer?

When investigators examine a computer during a trial or other formal proceedings, they can learn a great deal about the owner of the computer from many obscure sources that even the most sophisticated computer user may not think of. From an information security perspective, this also presents challenges when computers are broken into or stolen.

For example, words that a user has added to the custom dictionary in his or her word processing and email programs can reveal a lot about that person's business. A consultant may have added the names of clients, places, and products relating to their work, to avoid the annoyance of a spell-checker consistently tripping over them in word processing documents and email messages. These proper names and confidential data (along with industry jargon) are likely to be extremely important indeed, as they were used frequently enough to cause a spell-checking annoyance.

Electronic Discovery Planning Checklist

To prepare for the possibility of a discovery order covering electronic records, consider the following questions:

1) **Access.** Can electronic records and information be quickly and efficiently found and produced from the storage media and devices upon which they are stored? If not, consider revisiting retention plans, data center capabilities, indexing and searching methods, and characteristics of storage technology in use.

2) **Separation.** If "responsive" e-records (i.e., those relevant to the litigation) will be viewed in electronic form, can they be easily separated from "non-responsive" records and information? This is required to protect against the inadvertent disclosure of irrelevant information that may be proprietary or confidential, and to protect information subject to the attorney-client privilege and/or the attorney work product doctrine. If not, consider how system configuration or new technology investments may provide this functionality, by allowing several different "views" of information according to metadata, access privileges, and other search mechanisms and criteria.

3) **Long-term access.** Can records be preserved in such a way that they can be found, accessed separately, utilized, produced, and/or printed several years from now if required?

Have you accounted for media, software, and hardware obsolescence? These should be standard components of any Information Management program.

4) **Disposition.** Does your organization have outdated, unneeded information and records "lying around" that no longer need to be retained? Ensure that records disposition procedures account for the disposition of **all copies** of digital information.

An E-Discovery Scenario

Your corporate attorney asks you about the company's ability to search for and produce email messages. She needs some help responding to a request from a regulator regarding complaints about aggressive sales tactics targeted at the elderly, and wants to know what email records can be searched and found in the next two weeks.

Are you prepared to respond to her needs? In particular:

- Who would you contact to search and find the required email (called "responsive" email in legal terminology)?

- Do you know for certain what records exist and where to find them?

- Do you have a listing of computer systems, applications, and their administrators and locations within the company?

- Where would you start to look and whom could you assign to help?

- If you have to look in all company facilities in which servers or computers are located, which staffers at each location will do the looking?

- If employees are asked to look through their stored email and for responsive material, how much time will that take, and what will the cost be in terms of lost work, opportunity costs, and real hard costs?

> - Which employees could be pulled from their current duties to help search for needed email?
>
> - What contents are stored on back-up tapes, and how long are they retained?
>
> - With your company's current technology, can you search every place an email may be stored, and if not, what will you do or who will you rely upon for assistance?
>
> If you can't readily answer those questions, you should develop a more comprehensive and responsive electronic discovery plan.

Issue #3: Privacy

Private Information Is an Asset

You've likely received privacy policy statements from your bank, your stockbroker, and your creditors in the past year. And you have probably noticed that e-commerce websites publicize their privacy policies. Whether you've bothered to read any of them or not, you certainly know that privacy has become a prominent consumer issue. The personal information that banks, brokerage firms, creditors, e-merchants, and others collect about their customers is so valuable that other marketers are willing to pay tidy sums for such data. But consumers have become very protective of their private information.

One high-profile case to recently test the idea of private information as an asset was that of Toysmart.com. In 2001, this failed dot-com retailer allegedly listed the personal information of 250,000 customers as an asset that could be sold during bankruptcy proceedings. This, despite their privacy policy that stated:

> Personal information, voluntarily submitted by visitors to our site, such as name, address, billing information and shopping preferences, is never shared with a third party... When you register with Toysmart.com, you can rest assured that your information will never be shared with a third party.[96]

The customer data included details such as names, credit card information, home addresses, names and birthdays of children, and shopping preferences.

Following an outcry from former customers, privacy advocates, and a great deal of embarrassing coverage, their parent company agreed to buy the list for $50,000 and destroy it.

Privacy Policy Revisions

Internet retailer Amazon.com faced a similar outcry in 2001 when it allegedly made a change to its privacy policy that would allow it to sell its customer information to a third-party in the event that it was acquired or went out of business. The FTC launched an investigation into the way Amazon.com's change in its privacy policy affected consumers. Around the same time, Amazon paid up to $1.9 million to settle a class action lawsuit launched by users of the company's "Alexa" service who complained that personally identifiable information was being collected and retained in violation of the company's privacy policy. The FTC said that, "certain of Amazon.com's and Alexa Internet's practices likely were deceptive," and Amazon.com agreed to pay $40 to each affected user.

Organizations must ensure that their privacy policies are comprehensive enough to address all reasonably foreseeable events, like mergers, acquisitions, new business partners, and change in business direction. Also, organizations must be prepared to live by the promises made in these policies. If drastic changes are required, it may be necessary to "grandfather" existing customers under the old policy, while applying the new policy only to new customers. In any case, a proactive communication plan for all customers should be a prerequisite of any privacy policy change.

Ownership of Information

Your organization has a responsibility to properly manage and protect information assets as it would any other asset that it owns. The data stored on the information systems across your organization, from the largest customer relationship management databases to the smallest handheld email devices, are your organization's lifeblood, and must be protected as such.

The information that employees generate in their day-to-day working activities is also part of your organization's information asset collection. It is your responsibility to inform employees, through policies and training, that all such business information is the property of the organization. This will help to establish the importance of the information and set expectations for how this information will be treated when an employee leaves your organization. The following is a sample policy statement that informs employees about this issue.

Ownership of Company Information: Sample Policy Statement

All information that you create, receive, and/or use while conducting company business is owned by the Company, regardless of whether that information is in paper, electronic, or any other tangible form. In addition, all employees must provide all business information in their possession or control to the Company upon request, at any time, for any reason.

Individuals who cease to be employees of the Company must provide original and all copies of any business information to his or her supervisor prior to leaving the company. All business information located in any Company facility or facilities managed by another entity on behalf of the Company are presumed to be company property. All business information created or stored on or in a Company computer, imaging system, communications system, telecommunications system, storage device, storage medium, or any other Company system, medium, or device are presumed to be company property.

All business information, regardless of its location, that in any way pertains to the Company or Company business is presumed to be Company property. Only upon a showing that the business information in question does not in any way relate to Company business will such information be deemed to be other than company property. Theft or appropriation of any business information is strictly prohibited. Giving access to another person who is not authorized to have access to, review, or otherwise see company business information is also strictly prohibited.

Undertaking these prohibited acts may result in termination and/or civil or criminal penalties.

© 2004, Randolph A. Kahn, ESQ., and Barclay T. Blair. For informational purposes only. Seek the advice of counsel before adopting any Information Management policy element.

Privacy of Employee Information at Work

You need to be clear with employees about whether or not they should expect that the information they create and receive on the job is private. Generally speaking, organizations in the U.S. have taken the approach that such information is not private, and the organization thus reserves the right to access and review it at will.

U.S. courts have generally supported this approach. For example, in *Garrity v. John Hancock Mut. Life Ins. Co.*,[97] two female employees were fired for sending sexually explicit email over the company email system, in contravention of the company email policy. The employees viewed the email containing the offensive content as personal, and argued that the company invaded their privacy when it accessed and examined it. The court weighed the issues in order to determine if "the expectation of privacy was reasonable."

In this case, the court did not find that expectation reasonable, for several reasons:

- The company's email policy stated, "Company management reserves the right to access all Email files," and "there may be business or legal situations that necessitate company review of Email messages and other documents."

- The company "periodically reminded employees that it was their responsibility to know and understand the email policy," and employees had been warned about "several incidents in which employees were disciplined for violations."

- The two employees testified that they sent the email messages (some of which were jokes) to other employees with the expectation that they would subsequently be forwarded to others.

- The employees admitted that they knew the company had the ability to examine company email messages.

Legal opinions on this approach to employee privacy at work are not consistent in every jurisdiction, and companies should investigate the laws of each jurisdiction in which they do business. For example, the Social Chamber of the Supreme Court of France ruled in 2001 that an employee's personal email sent or received on company systems could not be accessed and viewed by an employer, even if the company advised employees that they would do so.

Privacy of Employee Information: Sample Policy Statement

Company resources used by employees to create, transmit, receive, and store business information, such as computers, the email system, and facsimile machines, should only be used for business purposes. In addition, the information in these systems should only be related to Company business. These resources, and the information contained within them, are the property of the Company. Furthermore, the company reserves the right to access and review any business information, whether it is located in company facilities or not.

Employees do not have and should not expect any right to privacy with respect to any Company business information, including email transmission, electronic communication, or Internet or intranet communication. The Company reserves the right to monitor the use of any company property, equipment, phone line, computer, software, or any storage device.

© 2004, Randolph A. Kahn, ESQ., and Barclay T. Blair. For informational purposes only. Seek the advice of counsel before adopting any Information Management policy element.

Issue #4: Protecting Company Information
Project Elvis and the Six Million Dollar Plan

One day in 2002, an executive who had founded the public finance division at a Memphis securities firm suddenly jumped ship to a competitor—and took nearly his entire division with him. His former employer alleged that he and other employees had stolen or destroyed thousands of documents and electronic files when they left, effectively decimating the operations of that division.[98]

The National Association of Securities Dealers (NASD) began an investigation. According to the NASD, the executive had been planning the defection—which he called "Project Elvis"—for nearly a year. They found a spreadsheet containing the titles that each defecting employee would have at the new firm, email discussions about compensation and other issues, and even digital photos of the executive's new office space.

Investigators completed an in-depth digital forensics exercise that included an examination of the employees' computers at their new jobs, laptops, dozens of pieces of removable media such as CDs, and also PDAs. The investigation revealed that the employees had allegedly pilfered a broad range of material, including Microsoft Outlook files, pricing documents, and transaction information. In addition they found hundreds of email messages that employees had apparently forwarded from their work email account to personal, Web-based email accounts.

The NASD awarded damages of $6 million to the securities firm, including nearly $400,000 in compensation that the executive had to return for the year he had spent conspiring with the competitor.

Lessons Learned

- Develop policies and procedures for departing employees—policies that establish that the company owns all information stored on company systems, and procedures that minimize the chance that employees will steal information when they leave.

- Immediately disable all network and email access when the employee is terminated, or at a predetermined time on the employee's last day. Instruct security personnel to develop procedures for quickly disabling network access for any employee at any time, as instructed by senior management.

- Use Information Management policies to inform employees that you reserve the right to monitor their use of corporate systems, including the email system.

- Your most valuable information may not be in paper form. Thousands of contacts and volumes of information can fit on a single CD, USB "memory stick," mobile email device, and numerous other media that can easily be slipped out of your facilities.

Issue #5: Disaster Recovery and Business Continuance

Although organizations have long prepared contingency plans designed to enable them to survive a disaster, after the events of 9/11, the concept of disaster recovery and business continuance has widened and become more complex. Today, it is clear that disaster recovery and business continuity concepts need to be a part of every Information Management program.

Moreover, contingency plans need to be constantly updated and adapted to account for new realities and risks. For example, when the SEC summarized the "Lessons Learned" by the financial industry after 9/11, they found that, although most Wall Street firms had back-up systems and data centers, many had not counted on the "wide-area" disaster of 9/11. As a result, some firms that had "arranged for their back-up facilities to be in nearby buildings… lost access to both their primary and back-up facilities in the aftermath."[99] Clearly, the events of 9/11 required all firms to revisit many aspects of their disaster recover plans to provide for greater geographic dispersion of back-up facilities, and many other elements that respond to newly understood disaster scenarios.

Many organizations found themselves in a similar situation following the blackouts in the northeastern North American in the fall of 2003—

in that their existing business continuance plans were not written to account for a power grid that requires $100 billion in modernization upgrades.[100]

IMC relies on disaster recovery and business continuance plans that protect business information and records. The best developed and maintained Information Management program is of little utility if the information assets that it is designed to manage are put at risk by an organization's failure to identify and respond to disasters and other risk factors that could cause large-scale loss of data, system outages, and other events that hamper an organization's ability to properly retain and manage business information.

Issue #6: Information Security

2003 Top Security Threats

1. Workplace Violence

2. Business Interruption/Continuity Planning

3. Internet/Intranet Security

4. Terrorism (Global and Domestic)

5. Employee Selection/Screening Concerns

6. Fraud/White-Collar Crime

7. General Employee Theft

8. Unethical Business Conduct

9. Drugs/Alcohol in the Workplace

10. Identity Theft

From "Top Security Threats and Management Issues Facing Corporate America, 2003 Survey of Fortune 1000 Companies," Pinkerton Consulting & Investigations Inc. © 2003 Used with permission.

Protecting your information assets can be a difficult task, requiring a complex mix of technology, policies, and people to combat expanding threats from viruses to hackers and everything in between. IMC depends on good information security practices, and there are several unique Information Management issues to consider, as explored below.

What Are We Trying to Protect?

There are several reasons why organizations need to implement security strategies for email. Failing to address security around our business information, including email, unnecessarily exposes organizations in all sorts of ways. Information security has a broad purpose that includes:

- Protect information from corruption

- Protect information from misappropriation and misuse

- Protect business operations

- Protect systems from interruptions, failures, and outages, and resulting loss of productivity

- Promote secure business

- Protect company reputation from bad publicity

- Promote confidence in leadership and company management

- Protect the integrity of company data

- Guard against loss or theft of property

- Prevent repudiation and unwinding of business transactions

- Protect the identities of business partners

- Protect different classes of company records including proprietary, trade secrets, and privileged and confidential communications

Managing Information Security Records

Information security systems create unique types of data that should be given special attention in your Information Management policies and procedures. Some data may require special handling procedures due to their complex or technical nature (e.g., encryption keys), and your Information Management program must account for this type of information. While special procedures may be required, you must ensure that such information is managed according to your established IMC principles, regardless of how unique the content or form of the information may be.

- Conduct an inventory of information security-related software and hardware used throughout your organization, such as encryption systems, firewalls, and user authentication modules.

- Work with IT/IS to determine what kind of information these technologies are generating or storing.

- Determine if any of this information meets your definition of a record. If so, establish a plan for the capture and retention of such information, which may include the creation of new categories for such information in organizational records retention rules.

- Remember that some information (firewall logs in the case of break-in, for example) may be required for litigation and other formal proceedings, and should be included in any Records Hold order related to such proceedings.

A good example of unique information security data is the records created by Public Key Infrastructure (PKI). PKI is a system of policies, people, and technology used to secure information systems. PKI uses advanced cryptography, and can be used for a variety of security-related purposes such as authenticating online identity, and protecting the confidentiality and integrity of information using encryption and digital signatures.

The records produced in the operation of a PKI include a variety of important policies, representations, contracts, and statements that have legal importance to the people and organizations that use and rely on transactions involving PKI. These include documents such as Certification Policies and Certification Practices Statements.

In providing guidance to organizations faced with the task of properly managing PKI records, NARA stated,

A key premise for this guidance is that PKI-unique administrative records do not constitute a new category of records that require a total "reinvention" of lifecycle Records Management policies and guidance. While the records a PKI produces may be unique in their content and application, the Records Management practices, as already embodied in certain federal statutes, regulations, guidance and standards, still apply.[101]

Road Warriors

Recent surveys indicate that over 80% of companies worldwide will have employees who telecommute by 2005.[102] In 2003, sales of notebook computers surpassed those of desktop computers.[103]

At the same time, analysts predict that there will be over 12,000 different physical locations (called hotspots) in the U.S. (70,000 worldwide) where road warriors can wirelessly connect to the Internet by the end of 2003, a number that will be five times higher by 2007.[104]

Although the benefits of telecommuting includes lower office overhead, improved morale, and boosted productivity,[105] companies must also be careful to consider the Information Management implications of this movement.

Mobile and remote workers present several unique IMC challenges you must address in policy and procedures, including:

- **Data protection.** Valuable data stored on mobile devices is more vulnerable to theft and loss than those stored inside the walls of the organization. Train employees to be aware that their laptop and PDA are targets for thieves. Airport security screening procedures post-9/11 that require the removal of these devices from carrying bags increase the risk of theft.

- **Retention.** You need a plan to ensure that information on mobile devices is routinely backed up or "synced" to your data center. There are a number of ways to securely perform remote back-ups to the corporate data center, which you should investigate with your IT/IS department. Data should not be retained or backed up on employees' home computers.

- **Unique records.** Mobile devices may create and retain data in proprietary or obscure formats that may not easily be handled by your Records Management systems. Ensure that data from such devices can be captured and retained in an accurate and reliable fashion before allowing employees to use such devices.

Do You Have a Laptop Problem?

Sales of laptop and notebook computers are outpacing sales of desktop computers.[106] Now is the time to look around your organization and see if you have a laptop problem.

Laptop computers can go anywhere, hold vast amounts of data, and can be connected wirelessly in an increasing number of public places. Those advantages can be an Information Management nightmare.

Are you addressing these issues?

- Ownership of data on laptop computers, especially if the computers are purchased by employees

- Loss resulting from theft of laptop computer containing proprietary company information

- Remote regular back-up of data for road warriors

- Information security policies for employees connected to public Internet and wireless terminals

- Finding and producing laptop content for litigation, audits, or investigations

- Personal use of laptop computers

- Installing and using only approved software on laptops

- Protection of confidential and trade secret information

Employee Use of Public Terminals

Maybe now you think that equipping employees with the latest and greatest laptops and portable devices isn't the best idea, and you should make road warriors use public Internet terminals like everyone else!

Not quite.

In 2003, a 24-year-old Queens, NY, man pled guilty to federal charges of computer damage, access-device fraud, and software piracy.[107] According to reports, the man had surreptitiously installed keylogging software on a number of Kinko's public Internet access terminals throughout Manhattan. The software enabled him to record each key pressed by customers accessing the Internet, including their passwords and a wealth of confidential and personal information. He then used that information to invade those customer's bank accounts, open new accounts in their names, and transfer funds to unauthorized accounts.

In this case, the hacker's plans seemed limited to using the stolen information to rob personal bank accounts. What if the motives were corporate espionage? What kind of information could he get from a Wall Street administrative assistant checking work email from an Internet café on a lunch break? Financial information? Company passwords? If he or she opened an email attachment containing a confidential presentation, for example, a copy of that file may be created on the public computer, even if the administrative assistant does not save it. And, a sophisticated criminal, such as our man in Queens, would know where to find it.

What can you do to protect against these security risks? One approach is to prohibit employees from using public computers for work purposes. If this is not practical, at a minimum, employees should receive training on the risks of using public terminals.

Patch Management

In the summer of 2003, organizations around the globe were hit with a double whammy. The W32.Blaster computer worm took advantage of operating system security vulnerabilities, and a virulent new form of the Sobig virus generated thousands of infectious email messages. Computers were disabled, airline flights were delayed, and some trains stopped running.[108]

For organizations in the northeastern U.S., which were also victims of power outages around the same time, it was an information security "perfect storm." In fact, there is evidence that the worm significantly hampered efforts to address the blackout.[109]

Patch Management (PM) is the art and science of keeping software up-to-date with the latest "patches"—pieces of computer code that fix a vulnerability, correct mistakes, improve functionality, and so on. While it may sound simple and neat, PM today is messy work. Allowing your antivirus software to automatically update itself on your personal computer is one thing—applying an operating system patch to 20,000 computers across the globe is another.

Organizations employ a variety of tools and techniques to help. For example, many vendors provide software that will automatically inform an IT department when updates are available for a specific piece of software, and then help them test and install that update across an enterprise.

In the case of the W32.Blaster worm, many people questioned why the worm was able to spread at all, given that the vulnerability, and the patch fixing the problem, had been released weeks before. This event served to highlight the many difficulties of PM.

Organizations with massive computer networks that support many different operating systems and complex customized software cannot simply install the latest patch without adequate testing—a process that may take weeks and months to complete. However, new vulnerabilities are discovered every day. According to the CERT Coordination Center (a non-commercial institution that tracks and advises on information security incidents globally), the number of software security vulnerabilities has doubled every year since 1999. In 2002, there were nearly 4,200 reported vulnerabilities.[110]

To address the gap, organizations apply risk management principles, weighing the damage potentially caused by the security vulnerability against the cost of testing and applying the patch. And to ease the pain of applying the patch, many organizations also employ change management techniques to ensure that their systems will not malfunction due to software changes caused by new patches (see page 249).

Aside from the inherent difficulties of PM, many organizations continue to be vulnerable simply because they have inadequate policies and procedures. Through lack of awareness, commitment, resources, or other reasons, increasingly, organizations without a PM plan are putting themselves, and other organizations, at risk.

Patch Management must be a part of your organization's Information Management Program.

Key #2

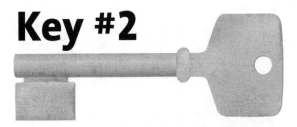

Executive-Level Program Responsibility

Senior executives and managers must take overall responsibility for the Information Management Program.

Key Overview

The success of any important organizational activity depends in large part on the commitment of the organization's senior management team. This commitment can be expressed in concrete ways, such as funding levels; and less tangible ways, such as making it a priority at the executive round table.

IMC is no different. A successful Information Management program requires senior executives and managers to step up and take responsibility for the program's development, implementation, and ongoing improvement.

Chapter 10:

Executive Leadership, Sine Qua Non[111]

IMC depends on executives and senior management taking responsibility for their organization's Information Management activities. Executive responsibility is more than just "optics" or keeping up appearances. Rather, as outlined in the Federal Sentencing Guidelines, high-level personnel in the organization "must have been assigned overall responsibility to oversee compliance with... standards and procedures." There are many reasons why executive involvement and responsibility is important for IMC, as this chapter explores.

Policy Comes from Above

Senior management is responsible for setting an organization's direction and communicating priorities to employees. High-level, visible executive involvement and responsibility makes clear that IMC is a priority for the organization and is central to its success. Practically speaking, without high-level involvement, employees across the organization may fail to take the initiative as seriously as they should, or they may ignore it altogether.

Policy direction must come from above to achieve the following objectives:

- **Consistency.** To create organization-wide consistency.

- **Resource allocation.** Business units will be reluctant to spend money complying with policy that is not tied directly to their budgets and management objectives unless the policy comes from the top.

- **Motivation.** Employees and managers are motivated to follow the directives of those who evaluate them, so unless the directives come from the top, only pockets of the organization may be motivated to follow the policies. Policy does not come from below.

- **Delegation.** Middle management is most effective at directing implementation, training, and enforcement tasks, not originating policy. Plus, there is little incentive for employees to listen to managers from outside their business group.

- **Influence.** Employees are less likely to listen to designated "policy makers" who lack sufficient authority to impose the change on the organization.

- **Accountability.** In the wake of corporate reform movements and laws like Sarbanes-Oxley, shareholders, boards, regulators, and auditors are looking to top management for assurances that information is being properly managed. Only the involvement of senior executives can provide this assurance.

Many Information Management initiatives fail for the simple reason that they were being advanced by personnel who did not have, or were perceived not to have, the support or authority of top management.

Senior Management's Responsibility

In *United States ex rel. Koch v. Koch Indus.*,[112] "certain computer tapes were destroyed by Koch's data processing personnel, at a time when Koch had a duty to preserve them."

Who was held to blame for this violation? The individuals in Data Processing? The court found that it was "due to the negligence of Koch's senior management."

Companies and Executives Pay the Price for Their Failures

The CEO and other senior executives are ultimately responsible for their organization's performance. In the case of a public company that can be measured by stock performance—if the stock is not performing, heads may begin to roll.

The first few years of this new millennium have illustrated time and again that a failure to properly manage records and information can have disastrous consequences—including a direct impact on a company's stock price. For example, reports of an FDA investigation into "fraudulent recordkeeping" at one of the world's largest pharmaceutical companies sent its shares to their lowest point in 12 months.[113]

In the last five years, Records Management, information security, disaster recovery, and a whole host of Information Management issues have been tied directly to a company's performance in the market.

Who Has Time for It?

The average worker today is increasingly being asked to do more. According to the International Labor Institute, 80% of American men and 64% of women now work overtime hours.[114] The pressures of productivity coupled with the rapid pace of technological and economic change mean that employees have less and less time for "non-core" activities (activities that are not directly related to their performance evaluation and compensation).

Unless senior management creates a culture that makes Information Management activities a core responsibility, employees have little practical incentive to take their responsibilities seriously. Employees have enough to do without worrying about activities that are perceived as "nice to have" as opposed to essential.

Organizational Culture

The so-called "star CEO" has taken a bit of a beating lately, with all the reports of excessive compensation packages and corruption coming out of the 1990s boom era and beyond. Still, the CEOs of many of our largest organizations are well-known public figures. And each CEO has a personality that is often reflected in the culture of his or her company.

Indeed, senior management is largely responsible for creating the culture and personality of an organization. If senior management is not shaping the personality of an organization, they are not doing their jobs.

Management shapes an organization's personality by the ethics, values, priorities, and strategies that it lays out and promotes in both conceptual and practical ways. For example, a culture of "employee flexibility" may be supported by job sharing, flexible hours, and onsite daycare. A culture of organizational accountability, transparency, and IMC must similarly be supported in real and practical ways: by statements of support from the top; by clear, accessible policies and procedures; by employee training; and by adequate funding.

In short, creating an organizational culture that considers Information Management a normal part of day-to-day business operations and part of every employee's job description is the responsibility of senior management.

It's Not Just the CFO

When companies are prosecuted for financial manipulation and fraud, it is not just the CFO who is targeted. Other members of the executive roundtable are often involved as well. For example, when the SEC brought action against a manufacturer for manipulating its financials, the VP of Finance as well as director and member of the audit committee, and the Chief Operating Officer were all charged with violations of securities laws. Many types of fraud and manipulation require the involvement of various parts of the business, such as this one, which involved booking revenue for goods that were not yet shipped, among other things.[115] Everyone at the executive table shares responsibility for Information Management.

Executive Responsibility for Preservation of Evidence

In the case of *In re Prudential Ins. Co. of America Sales Practices Litigation*,[116] Prudential was fined $1 million for a failure to preserve evidence relevant to the case, and the court squarely placed the blame on the shoulders of senior management.

Excerpts from the decision:

"Prudential top management… recognized that the sales practices lawsuits and regulatory investigations are an extremely important part of Prudential's business… more importantly, they all recognized Prudential's obligation to preserve documents in connection with the lawsuits and investigations. Yet, none took an active role in formulating, implementing, communicating, or conducting a document retention policy."

"When the [preservation order] was entered, it became the obligation of senior management to initiate a comprehensive document preservation plan and to distribute it to all employees."

"When senior management fails to establish and distribute a comprehensive document retention policy, it cannot shield itself from responsibility because of field office actions. The obligation to preserve documents that are potentially discoverable materials is an affirmative one that rests squarely on the shoulders of senior corporate officers."

Fighting the Tide Is a Job for Someone Strong

Too few companies consider the IMC implications of new technology before they implement the technology. As a result, too many organizations have suffered damage that resulted from improper employee use or abuse of information systems. Efforts to address Information Management problems too often only occur reactively, after the damage has been done.

Instead, IMC should be a proactive effort that identifies and address-es problems before they occur—an approach that is likely to be less expensive and more effective in the long run. Only senior manage-ment can create the organizational culture that will ensure that a proactive approach is taken.

Before implementing new technology, senior management should ensure that the organization has asked the right questions. These questions include:

- What are the risks of using and misusing the technology?

- What is the likelihood that employees will misuse the tech-nology?

- What is the potential harm to the company if they do misuse the technology?

- Are there any regulatory directives to manage the technolo-gy or its output (information, data, or records)?

- Should the company retain the information, data, or e-record from the system for any business, operational, or administra-tive purposes?

- What can the company do to minimize misuse and liability?

- Do we have policies that tell employees what to do and what not to do?

- Do we have procedures that deal with the details of retention and storage?

- Which senior executive will "own" the process of informing employees about the rules and what is expected of them?

- Who will write rules, and how will the rules get disseminated?

- Who will train the employees?

- Who will audit the system?

- Who will discipline the offenders?

Consistency Across Lines-of-Business

Having the highest level of management make clear that IMC is a priority throughout the entire organization is imperative to ensure that all business units take action in a uniform and timely manner. Because in many organizations business units are semi-autonomous, direction must come from the very top in order to create consistency across all the units. Directives from peer business units are less likely to be successful.

On a recent visit to a business unit that is part of a large client organization, the Records Manager told us that the entire organization's Records Management directives came from his operation, not from the parent company. He admitted that only one business unit was following those directives, because they were not considered high priority. Although the program had its strong points, it was essentially rendered worthless by the perception that it was voluntary, because the directives were created by and disseminated from a peer business unit. Even worse, a court could find that having a policy and not following it is worse than not having one at all. So the organization was putting itself at real risk. Creating the policy indicates that the organization thought the issue was important; therefore it will be difficult to claim that lack of awareness is what caused the failure. In any event, it was clear that consistent adherence to records directives was not going to happen without a major nudge from a "C-level" executive.

Eventually the company got the message, and the CFO and general counsel provided the impetus for the organization as a whole to rethink Records Management when confronted with the reality that one small records problem could strip billions of dollars of market value from their public company, as they had observed happening to companies around them.

Information Management Vendor Choices

Employees may think that they have done their organization a service by negotiating a "cheap" deal with an Information Management vendor. However, executives should understand that "cheap" might be "expensive."

Nowhere is this truer than in Information Management, where an organization's information assets can disappear in a flash.

For example, in *Mobil Oil Corporation v. Grinnell Corporation*,[117] Mobil was awarded $20.7 million in compensation for the loss of 68,000 boxes of records that were destroyed by fire at their records storage vendor's warehouse. In all, more that 800,000 boxes of records were destroyed in the fire, and another plaintiff was awarded $20.5 million in compensation. Why were so many records destroyed? The court found that the sprinkler system in the warehouse was never completed, and even if it had been, it would not have been capable of controlling the fire.

Perhaps the "price was right" for the employee who negotiated the deal with the records vendor. But the damage to the company made the deal seem very expensive.

Executives must set the tone (as well as the example) for employees who have responsibility for negotiating deals with vendors where Information Management is at stake. That is, skimping on the quality of the service to save pennies today could cost the company dearly tomorrow.

Put Your Money Where Your Mouth Is

IMC is an enterprise-wide effort, one that affects all business units individually and collectively. Overall responsibility for ensuring that these efforts are adequately funded and staffed resides with senior management.

A failure to adequately fund an Information Management program will not only contribute to its demise, but will also send the message to employees, board members, and shareholders that the organization does not take Information Management seriously.

Giving a peer business unit responsibility for the Information Management program across the organization is typically a recipe for disaster, as these units do not have control of the budget—which makes it difficult to exercise any real control or to influence the process.

The Economics of Top-Level Coordination

Top-level coordination encourages efficient use of resources and eliminates duplication of effort and technology resources. It would clearly be inefficient, for example, for each business unit in an organization to license and operate a different document management or email system.

Consider the following example: The IT department of a company, without consulting the CIO, purchased a document management application for the entire enterprise. As it turned out, the application failed to address the needs of one particular business unit. So the company had to invest in a separate application to provide that single business unit the functionality it needed. The total cost for the two applications was nearly double the cost of the first application. If the executives of all the business units had been engaged in the original procurement process, the application could have been designed to serve all business units, for not much more cost than the original application.

Uniform technology implementation encourages consistency and efficiency; volume buying also results in better pricing.

Having CIO "oversight" of purchasing and implementation issues helps to ensure that technology will be uniform across disparate business units, which also can increase the success of an Information Management program.

Can the CEO Really Be Held Accountable for Information Management?

The chief executive of an organization bears ultimate responsibility for IMC, and may be held accountable by the courts. This was illustrated clearly in *Danis v. USN Communications*,[118] a shareholder class action suit that addressed senior management's failure to properly manage information prior to and during litigation. The company mismanaged records and improperly destroyed information, putting the court in the position of determining which individuals were to blame.

The court found that the CEO:

1) As "head of day-to-day management... had the **authority** and **responsibility** to implement a suitable document preservation program"

2) "Was at fault for **delegating** that function to a person who **lacked** the experience to perform that job properly"

3) "Further was at fault for **failing** to exercise any ongoing **oversight** to ensure that the job was done properly" [emphasis added throughout]

As a result, the court fined the CEO $10,000 to "impress upon [him] the seriousness of the duty of preservation, and to deter others from failing to properly discharge that duty."

This case is a great example for all organizations to study, as it provides insight into the type of expectations that the law has regarding the Information Management responsibilities not only of CEOs, but also of boards and middle management.

Specific Issues for the CEO

The court in *Danis* went on to detail its view of how the CEO and the management team failed in its Information Management obligations.

1) **No active management.** The CEO "personally took no affirmative steps to ensure that the [document retention] directive was followed."

2) **No preservation policy.** He did not direct that the company "implement a written, comprehensive document preservation policy, either in general or with specific reference to the lawsuit."

3) **No notice of the need to suspend normal policies.** "He did not instruct that any email or other written communication be sent to staff to ensure that they were aware of the lawsuit and the need to preserve documents."

4) **No supervision.** He "did not meet with the department heads after this staff meeting to follow up to see what they had done to implement the document preservation directive."

5) **Improper delegation.** He "exhibited extraordinarily poor judgment" by delegating these responsibilities to an in-house attorney with no litigation experience nor experience in developing a retention program, especially when he had the option of using an outside law firm with deep experience in these issues. Delegation is covered in detail in Chapter 13.

In-House Counsel's Responsibility

The CEO was not the only one blamed by the court for the company's Information Management failures. The in-house attorney was criticized because:

1) **No employee notice.** He did "nothing to ensure that all... employees who handled documents that might be discoverable were aware of the lawsuit and the need to preserve documents."

2) **No employee meetings.** He "held no meetings with employees below the managerial level."

3) **No written communication.** He "did not issue any written communications to anyone on the subject."

4) **No supervisory follow-up.** He "did nothing to determine whether the managers who attended the staff meeting followed his direction of communicating to their respective departments the need to preserve documents."

5) **No policy review.** He "did not review the pre-existing practices… relating to document preservation for terminated employees and closed offices, to determine whether these practices were still suitable in light of the need to preserve documents as a result of litigation."

The Role of the Board

Even the company's board did not escape blame from the court for the company's Information Management failures. The court faulted the company's board of directors for not taking "any active role in implementing a broader preservation policy," and for not following up with the CEO "to determine if their directive had been implemented."

The court in *Danis* went even further, criticizing the "hands-off" approach of the board:

> The outside directors believed that taking an active role in ensuring preservation of documents was not part of their "responsibility as director[s]," but that "[t]he people down in the trenches who gathered the data" would perform that task. This myopic view begs the question of who was supposed to see to it that the "people down in the trenches" actually carried out the task.

In the wake of Sarbanes-Oxley, it is even riskier for a board to take such an approach today.

Executive Checklist

■ Routinely and outwardly support the Information Management initiative.

■ Clarify your expectations.

■ Delegate important tasks to the right senior people. Clarify who should take responsibility for the success of specific initiatives.

■ Document your support of Information Management program through presentations, memos, email, voicemail "blasts," webcasts, etc.

■ Adequately fund Information Management initiatives.

■ Make clear that Information Management directives apply to, and affect the performance of, all employees and all business units.

Chapter 11:

What Executive Responsibility Means

In the previous chapter, we examined why executive leadership and responsibility is so critical to the success of compliant Information Management programs. In this chapter we will discuss practical ways in which executives can exercise this leadership role.

Creating a Culture of Information Management Awareness

There are several things that senior executives can do to get the message across to all employees that IMC is important to the organization, is a core part if its day-to-day operations, and is central to its success.

The CEO Statement

Many organizations include a statement or introductory letter from the CEO, Chief Operating Officer, or other high-level executive, as part of the employee orientation manual. This statement may also introduce a Records Management policy, appear on the intranet site that houses Information Management policies and procedures, and be inserted in an email reminder. Whatever the vehicle, it is important that the employee get the message from an executive.

Although the text of such a statement will naturally vary from organization to organization, its basic elements are as follows:

1) Records and information are valuable assets that the company relies upon for a variety of business and legal purposes.

2) Properly managing information is central to the organization's success.

3) The Information Management program is designed to ensure that this information is available when the company needs it.

4) The company complies with all laws and regulations regarding records and information.

5) It is each employee's responsibility to assist in ensuring that information is properly managed.

6) Failure to comply with Information Management policies and procedures will not be tolerated in any employee or executive.

A Sample CEO Statement

Dear Associates,

As you may already know, our company generates a great deal of information. In fact, we generate and use so much information each day that you could say that information is the lifeblood of our business. Each day, for example, our company generates about 100,000 email messages, and creates more than 50,000 MB of digital information (about 700 hard drives). This is in addition to the thousands of paper documents that we receive and process.

Much of this information has business, operational, legal, and historical importance, and as such must be properly managed. This is a responsibility that we all share. We depend on this information to better serve our customers, to plan and forecast, and to meet our legal and regulatory obligations. Managing this information effectively is central to our success; failing to manage it can result in severe penalties, reduced profitability, and disciplinary action.

All of us are responsible for helping to manage and protect our valuable business information, and to dispose of it only when directed in accordance with written policy. This is why we have created our Records Management Manual and its related policies—to ensure that we all understand how to properly manage and use that information throughout our organization.

Regards,

The CEO

The Executive Information Management Council

Once senior management has decided to make IMC a high priority, the next logical step is to turn over execution of the program to an experienced group of senior personnel. It is critical that this group, which makes things happen on a day-to-day basis, be assembled with care. As the *Danis* case makes clear, the court will not tolerate delegation of important activities to unqualified individuals. In addition, Information Management is a multi-disciplinary activity that requires the right mix of people and expertise to ensure full compliance.

The precise makeup and responsibilities of this group will vary by organization, but many organizations may want to create an Executive Information Management Council. This Council would have organization-wide responsibility for ensuring that the Information Management program is properly implemented throughout the company, and that needed policies and procedures are in place to address operational, legal, and technical needs and requirements.

The Council might include representatives from the following departments:

- Legal
- Human Resources
- Information Technology

- Finance

- Records Management

- Business Risk Management

- Tax and Audit

- Compliance

- Leadership from affected business units

It may also be helpful to provide a mechanism for "end-user" input. The Council should have the ability to create subordinate committees to address specific Information Management issues at a top level of the organization, and also to coordinate with similar councils within business units. Other considerations in forming the Council include:

- **Size.** The Council members should represent a broad cross-section of the company, to ensure that the concerns of all business units are considered; but small enough to get the job done in an efficient and timely way, without getting bogged down in bureaucratic minutiae.

- **Authority.** The Council should be granted enough authority to make things happen.

- **Charter.** The Council's activities and mandate should be broad enough to ensure that all major issues are addressed, but defined narrowly enough that it can address real, practical issues.

What Happens to Records When Executives Leave the Organization?

Organizations must ensure that they retrieve all information and records from departing employees. This is especially important with executives and senior management, who often have the organization's "keys to the kingdom" in their possession, whether in paper files or on their computers. Aside from confidentiality, privacy, privilege, trade secret, and other issues, organizations may need information held by executives to defend the organization in court and to respond to investigations and audits.

In the case of *In Re Three Grand Jury Subpoenas Duces Tecum*,[119] the government was investigating an organization for criminal "falsification of the corporation's books and records" and other charges. The corporation pled guilty to "to making false entries in its books and records," and agreed to cooperate with the ongoing investigation.

During the investigation, two officers who worked in the division where the wrongdoing allegedly took place left the organization and one of them signed a severance agreement saying he would cooperate with the investigation after he left the organization.

Years later, the government issued a subpoena to 12 former employees, demanding "any and all records, documents, instructions, memoranda, notes and papers (whether in computerized or other form) in [their] care, custody, possession or control, that were created during the course of, or in connection with, your employment at [the corporation]." The two former officers refused to produce the information, claiming that they were protected by the Fifth Amendment's protection against self-incrimination. Although the government argued that the officers continued to act as the custodians of the records even after their employment ended, the court found that once an officer leaves an organization, he or she is acting in a personal capacity and therefore can be protected from producing incriminating organization records in their possession by the Fifth Amendment.

In other cases, such as *Gloves, Inc. v. Berger*,[120] the law has been interpreted differently. In this case the court found that a custodian of corporate records continues to hold them in his or her capacity as a former representative of the organization, not in a personal capacity, "thus, production of such documents is required regardless of whether the custodian is still associated with the corporation." Other cases have come to similar conclusions.

Many of these problems can be avoided if organizations implement and consistently enforce a clear policy that requires all records in "the possession, custody, or control" of executives to be returned to the organization before the executive's employment is terminated. In the case of executives, companies should consider making this part of a standard employment contract.

Chapter 12:

IT Leadership

Sarbanes-Oxley is reverberating throughout IT management like an eerie echo of Y2K, with compliance deadlines looming and businesses feeling threatened and uncertain about the extent of the potential damage (that is, legal trouble) if changes aren't made.[121]

Computerworld, June 2003

In the wake of recent laws and regulations aimed at corporate reform and accountability, such as the Sarbanes-Oxley Act of 2002, Chief Information Officers (CIOs) and their departments are taking responsibility for not only their organization's technology systems, but also for the information stored within those systems. Some view this as an inevitable evolution: it only makes sense that those who "own" the IT systems would be the best people to take responsibility for their contents. To others, the evolution is not so clear and they see trouble ahead.

What is clear is that business and IT executives often see the world very differently. For example, a recent survey conducted by RoperASW of U.S. executives found very different attitudes on disaster recovery. While only 14% of business executives felt they would be "very vulnerable" to data loss in the event of a disaster, 54% of IT executives felt the same way.[122] Which executive knows the real story? Internal confusion and a lack of communication at the executive level do not bode well.

In many ways, Sarbanes-Oxley is the perfect illustration of the way that IT and business executives may be forced together in ways never imagined before. The law, with its focus on "internal controls" designed to guarantee the accuracy of financial information, among other things, is in many ways a "shotgun marriage" between technological and management controls. As a result, if the CIO didn't already have a seat at the table, in an increasing number of organizations you can be sure that he or she will.

IT Leadership Is Changing

The role of CIOs and other IT executives is changing (or should be changing) in many organizations to reflect our increasing reliance upon digital information for business purposes, and for transactions that have profound legal and regulatory ramifications. The popular view of IT as a service bureau that offers "commodity" information services to the rest of the company is too limited when one considers the staggering growth of technologies like email. Analysts estimate that the volume of business email is growing at a rate of 300% a year, and that the average employee creates 5 MB of email content each day.[123] Much of that daily 5 MB has real business, operational, legal, regulatory, and/or historical significance and must be retained and managed properly.

Obviously, a big challenge today for any big IT department is coping with the sheer volume of information passing through and being processed and stored by the systems that it controls. To make matters worse, the courts have placed a higher value on the need to retain certain kinds of records than on IT's need to run a cost-effective operation. This was made clear in *Applied Telematics v. Sprint*,[124] as previously alluded to, where a company was penalized for destroying information relevant to the litigation by overwriting the back-up tapes that contained the information.

At the same time, the courts and many regulators are taking a closer look at the way organizations manage digital information. Instant Messaging has evolved into a serious enterprise tool. The regulators have taken notice of this evolution, and in the securities industry have made clear that Instant Messages need to be retained by firms like any other piece of business correspondence.[125]

Digital Information Is Changing

More and more of the information generated and received by organizations has serious legal and regulatory ramifications. This information, such as digital contracts, invoices, patient data in healthcare, and order flow information in securities, has different storage and management needs than much of the other information generated by organizations. This kind of information is often referred to as "fixed" content that must be stored in a way that preserves its original form and content to comply with records and evidentiary requirements.

In addition, fixed content may need to be:

- Stored for longer periods of time than information that is more transitory,

- Stored in a way that can withstand an attack on its credibility or trustworthiness, and

- Accessed in a variety of ways by a variety of users.

Some analyst groups predict that storage of this kind of information will drive an increasing amount of overall IT storage budgets in the foreseeable future. According to Enterprise Storage Group, spending on services, software, and hardware for storing information with a view to compliance will exceed $6 billion between 2003 and 2007. This group also estimates that overall capacity required for storing compliant information will grow at a compound annual rate of 64% between 2003 and 2006.[126]

Dealing with Third-Party Providers

With companies increasingly using third-party storage vendors such as application service providers (ASPs) and storage services providers (SSPs), the question arises: How does outsourcing record storage affect the organization's responsibility to preserve and produce information for a lawsuit, audit, or investigation?

In most situations, just because records are not in your facility or in onsite computers does not mean you are no longer responsible for preserving them or making them available. If a vendor is acting on your behalf according to a contract, you better make sure they are doing exactly what you would do if the records were stored on your premises—or you might end up paying for their mistakes.

How to protect your organization when a third-party is involved:

- Make sure that you, not the storage vendor, set retention rules for your records at their facility or in their computers. Your two organizations will have different exposure to liability in event of retention failure, so your motivation to properly retain information comes from different sources.

- Ensure that you have a mechanism in place to notify the vendor of an anticipated, filed, or ongoing investigation, audit, litigation, and/or other formal proceedings that may require special preservation or production of information in their systems.

- Ensure that the vendor is contractually bound to cooperate with your requests for retrieval and production on your schedule, not theirs.

- Create clear contractual responsibilities delineating what happens if and when the relationship ends—your information is in their control and you are relying on their software and hardware.

- Ensure that adequate documentation of these activities is created and retained.

The Impact of Sarbanes-Oxley on IT/IS Management

Although Sarbanes-Oxley is aimed directly at public companies, all organizations need to pay attention to the law's emphasis on internal controls. Simply put, organizations cannot have confidence that their electronic records are trustworthy without also being sure that the IT systems that house and manage those records are trustworthy. The impact of Sarbanes-Oxley on IT/IS management extends beyond the precise dictates of the law because, in many ways, Sarbanes-Oxley has ushered in an era where IT/IS is increasingly "regulated." An era where IT must be managed with a view not only to technical performance and efficiency, but also to the impact of an ever-increasing range of laws and regulations. The chart of questions below illustrates the shift in thinking that is required in those who manage IT as a result of this changing landscape.

Questions IT/IS asked yesterday	New questions IT/IS should ask today
Is our data available to those who need it, when they need it?	Is our data trustworthy and reliable, and is it acceptable to our regulators and auditors?
How much time and money can we save if we reuse email back-up tapes every 30 days?	How big is the fine going to be when the court finds that we destroyed email evidence during the course of an investigation?
How can we make sure that our financial systems are always available?	How can we make sure that the financial reports our CEO signs are accurate, so we can keep him or her out of trouble?
Are electronic records admissible in court?	Do our electronic records have enough integrity and trustworthiness to be persuasive in court?
How much business will we lose if a virus or worm cripples our systems and those systems are unavailable to customers and suppliers?	How much money will the court award our customers and suppliers in damages when a virus or worm from our system cripples their systems?
What controls and procedures are going to help us maximize our storage and system resources?	What controls and procedures are going to ensure that e-records are retained in a trustworthy manner, for the length of time required by law or business needs?

Questions IT/IS asked yesterday	New questions IT/IS should ask today
How can we provide our employees with efficient access to databases and other repositories of company information?	How can we provide regulators, auditors, and the courts with access to the e-records and e-evidence that they require in a timely fashion, in a format they require, without exposing or releasing unrelated information?
How can we design our Web application to minimize calls to the help desk?	How can we design our Web application to capture a complete record of all user interactions for regulatory purposes?

The Total Cost of Failure (TCF)

In the technology world, there are typically two formal reasons given for purchasing new software or hardware.

1) To save money (i.e., by cutting costs through automation)

2) To make money (i.e., by creating new capabilities and opportunities)

In reality, the reasons that organizations buy particular software and hardware are much more complex. Purchasers may be driven by company culture, trends, fear, a good relationship with the vendor, or reasons that aren't exactly clear to anyone.

Whatever the case, it is clear that the formal reasons given typically change according to economic conditions. During the boom years of the 1990s, technology purchases were all about "sustainable competitive advantage," "leveraging synergies," and "the new economy."

In the economic downturn and general slowdown in the technology industry experienced in the first few years of the new century, technology buyers have become much more conscious of the bottom line, as they have in past downturns. In times like these, buyers begin to demand that new technology pay for itself in a reasonable timeframe.

There are many methods—some simple, some complex—for calculating whether or not a technology purchase will pay for itself. At their most complex, these calculations treat technology like an economic investment whose value can be determined using the same methods as those used for financial market options. On the other hand, the calculations can be as simple as this:

> If I buy this robot for $200,000, it will allow me to eliminate one human employee that now costs me $50,000 each per year. Therefore, the robot will start to save me money in the fifth year. And, I won't have to supply any coffee.

Of course, very few technology purchases are that simple, as the cost of ongoing maintenance for the robot, electricity, training for robot technicians, the serviceable life of the robot, union negotiations, lowered employee morale, and numerous other "hard" and "soft" factors would need to be calculated in order to get an accurate economic picture of the robot purchase.

Two of the most common models for calculating the economic feasibility of technology are "Return on Investment," or ROI, and "Total Cost of Ownership," or TCO. In their simplest application, these models are based on determining and predicting all the economic benefits of implementing new technology, and subtracting all the real and potential costs of the new technology, to determine whether the technology is a good idea economically.

$$\frac{\text{Total economic benefit}}{\text{Time}} - \frac{\text{Total economic cost}}{\text{Time}} = \frac{\text{Positive/negative \$}}{\text{Time}}$$

Total Cost of Ownership, then, is one method of calculating the economic consequences of taking the action of buying, implementing, and maintaining new technology.

TCF—Turning the Model on Its Head

One of the most common complaints heard from people involved in Information Management is that it is difficult to economically justify the expenditures necessary to "do it right." There is a seemingly constant battle between those in the company that see the risks of IMC failure, and those who hold the purse strings. Business managers are not typically rewarded for spending money on projects for which there are no easily understood economic benefits.

Although the reluctance to spend money on Information Management has changed somewhat as a result of the current business climate with its never-ending parade of news stories about corporate malfeasance, organizations need an easy and consistent way to understand the economics of Information Management Compliance.

This is where our concept of Total Cost of Failure, or TCF, comes in. TCF turns TCO on its head.

Whereas TCO is about calculating the economics of taking action, TCF is about calculating the economics of failing to take action, or of taking the wrong actions.

As with calculating TCO, calculating TCF is not a science, and requires organizations to make educated guesses about possible cost sources in the future, the likelihood of particular cost sources occurring, the dollar amounts attached to various cost sources, and other factors.

Determining TCF Cost Sources

The costs associated with Information Management failure can come from many "hard" and "soft" sources. In order for a TCF estimate to be valuable, it must include consideration of the full range of possible costs.

By taking even a brief look at one aspect of Information Management—electronic discovery—it becomes clear the sources of cost that add up to TCF are varied and can add up very quickly (see page 108 for more information on electronic discovery).

What is the potential Total Cost of Failure of not having an adequate base of technology and policies to respond to the requests of the courts, regulators, auditors, and other parties for electronic records and other information?

- **Search and retrieval costs.** In the past, courts have required organizations to search through massive volumes of email, at great cost, to find information responsive to litigation.

- **New software.** Organizations may be required to buy special software or even develop their own software that will allow their data to be searched, compiled, copied, and/or translated into a different format.

- **Penalties for destruction of evidence.** The courts take such destruction of evidence very seriously, and as we have seen throughout this book, criminal and civil litigation can result.

- **Employee time lost** to participating in e-discovery efforts. This "soft cost" can in fact be the source of greatest expense, as dozens of IT and other staff are tied up in the discovery effort.

- **Forensic experts** for data recovery and testimony.

- **Technology experts** for custom coding.

- **Computers**, servers, and networks taken offline, or made unavailable.[127]

TCF Sources of Both "Hard" and "Soft" Costs

- Inconvenience to business and personnel

- Lost employee time

- Impact to system functionality

- Loss of customer confidence

- Lost organizational reputation

- Cost of losing a claim, dispute, lawsuit, audit

- Court-imposed sanctions and penalties

- Lost business or business opportunity

- Business failure

- Regulator's penalties and increased scrutiny

Quantifying TCF Risk

Information Management failures come in all shapes and sizes, from the innocuous to the catastrophic, occurring infrequently or on a regular basis. Central to assessing TCF is being able to assess the risk associated with a particular IMC failure, such as failing to comply with a regulation or not being able to locate information required to serve a customer's needs.

Quantifying risk is an art and science unto itself, but basic models, such as the one described below, can be employed to develop a useful profile of potential IMC failures and support decision-making processes.

There are three key variables that organizations should assess when considering the TCF of particular IMC failures, as follows:

1. Likelihood

On scale of 1-10 (1 being very unlikely, 10 representing certainty of failure) what is likelihood of experiencing a particular IMC failure?

2. Frequency

On a scale of 1-10 (1 meaning the failure would only occur once, 10 meaning the event is certain to occur periodically) how often would your organization experience the IMC failure?

3. Magnitude

On a scale of 1-10 (1 being inconsequential damage, 10 meaning catastrophic damage) what would the magnitude of the failure be?

Organizations can employ this model to measure the risk related to a particular IMC failure, and use this measurement to establish an acceptable threshold of risk for potential IMC failures. Although this threshold will naturally vary by organization, in general, a result of 18 or over on this scale should be enough to cause most organizations to investigate ways that the risk can be addressed and mitigated.

The Risk Model at Work: An Example

A fictional scenario that draws from real world scenarios can be used to illustrate how the TCF risk model may be used to help organizations in the IMC decision-making process.

In this scenario, a brokerage company wants to assess the potential risk of failing to retain and manage email communications in accordance with SEC regulations. The firm has already calculated TCO for the hardware, software, training, maintenance, and other costs of buying and implementing a Records Management system that will enable them to comply with the regulations. However, they are interested in establishing a useful quantification of the risk associated with not purchasing the system. The TCF Risk model outlined above can help the firm with this exercise.

1. Likelihood

Question: What is the likelihood that a regulator will unearth the noncompliance and penalize the brokerage company for failing to properly retain and manage the email?

Analysis. In the current business climate and given past SEC and NASD actions related to email retention and management failures (see page 83 for more information), the likelihood of uncovering the failure seems relatively high.

Estimated Risk: 8

2. Frequency

Question: How often will the firm's failure to retain and properly manage email cause harm to the firm?

Analysis. Until corrected, the activity will be the source of regulatory problems with the SEC, NASD, NYSE, and perhaps several state regulators. Additionally, their failure can be used against the firm in the context of litigation unrelated to these regulators. For example, in the context of litigation, the firm could be sanctioned for failing to retain records of business activities in accordance with the law, or for allowing email evidence to be destroyed. The event is likely to harm the firm repeatedly until it is corrected, and may even continue to harm the firm after corrective action is taken.

Estimated Risk: 9

3. Magnitude

Question: What is the extent of the damage, costs, and other harm likely to be if the firm is found to be failing to comply with the email retention and management regulations?

Analysis. Given that several brokerage companies have already been fined millions for the same IMC failure, it seems reasonable to expect that the direct costs of penalties could well be in the millions of dollars. Additionally, the costs of correcting the problem in real costs (software, hardware, training, etc. costs will likely be higher because correcting the problem in a reactive mode may not allow for competitive bidding), inconveniencing employees, and disrupting business may be even higher. Bad press may even be more harmful as investors and boards lose confidence in leadership, negatively impacting stock values.

Estimated Risk: 9

Overall Analysis

With an measurement of 26 (8-Likelihood, 9-Frequency, 9-Magnitude) the risk associated with failing to comply with the email retention and management regulations is very high, and indicates that the firm would be prudent to take action to prevent this failure from occurring.

Quantifying TCF in the Real World

1. A financial services company fails to preserve records for a pending lawsuit and the court penalizes the company $1 million and imposes an onerous preservation regime on the company costing untold sums and inconveniencing a workforce of tens of thousands.

In re Prudential Ins. Co. of America Sales Practices Litigation[128]

2. A company fails to follow its own disaster recovery back-up tape schedule. As a result it is confronted with a discovery expense of $6.2 million.

Murphy Oil USA, Inc. v. Fluor Daniel, Inc.[129]

3. Company records are burned in a third party's records center fire and as a result the company losses millions of dollars in tax write offs, among other damage sustained. Company awarded in excess of $20 million.

Mobil Oil Corporation v. Grinnell Corporation and Diversified Information Technologies Inc.[130]

Another Example: Verizon and the Slammer Worm

> *With respect to its actions taken to prevent or minimize worm attacks, we find that Verizon did not take all reasonable and prudent steps available to it... Thus, Verizon should be held accountable for its failure.*
>
> *Maine Public Utilities Commission Order*[131]

Verizon, a telecommunications company, had service agreements to provide network services to several other telcos such as AT&T and WorldCom (now called MCI). According to these agreements, Verizon would pay a penalty to its customers if the availability of its networks fell below 99.5%.

According to the Commission adjudicating the matter, in January 2003, an Internet worm known as the "Slammer Worm," which can damage and severely degrade online performance, hit Verizon's Internet servers. Verizon took its network services offline for about a day and a half in order to remove the worm and to test and apply a security patch from Microsoft that would protect against further attacks.

During this time, network services were unavailable to Verizon's customers, resulting in a level of service that fell below agreed-upon standards. AT&T and WorldCom therefore argued that they should receive a rebate as stipulated in the agreement. However, Verizon argued that the Slammer Worm was an "extraordinary event" and "unforeseen circumstance" that they had no control over, so there should be no rebate.

In its ruling the telecommunications commission found that the patch to protect against the Slammer Worm had been available for "at least six months before the attack actually occurred," and Microsoft had "issued 'Critical' security bulletins and associated software patches at both six and three months intervals prior to the event. Despite these warnings, Verizon apparently chose not to install the appropriate patch."

As such, the commission sided with Verizon's disgruntled customers and awarded the rebate at a cost to Verizon of:

1) $62,000 cash rebate;

2) Loss of customer goodwill; and,

3) Precedent set by the decision means that the company will need to reevaluate its procedures for securing and maintaining its systems, which could result in costs such as consultants, new technology, and more staff.

Lessons Learned

Industry experts have commented that the next round of "asbestos-type" class action litigation (i.e., massive settlements, worldwide, lasting for years, industry changing) could come from liability caused by information security breaches. It's commonplace for a virus to seize control of employees' contacts list and transmit and self-propagate their own virus by making it look like the email and attachment (which contains the virus) came from a known contact or colleague. The virus spreads like wildfire and impacts your customers' networks and computer without you even knowing about it.

- Costs for failure can come from unexpected sources. With the law still evolving on many issues around cyber-liability, organizations should be careful to consider all the risks from security failures. In addition to this case, there are other cases where organizations have suffered because of their own, or a partner or customer's, failure to maintain and secure their systems.

- Make sure that policies and procedures for applying security patches satisfy not only the technical needs for testing and interoperability, but also the legal need to protect against the liability that can come from security failures.

- Find out if there are points in your networks or systems that could be open to security failures that could create liability for your organization.

- Reevaluate agreements with Application Service Providers and other parties with whom you have service and perform-ance-based contracts. Do these contracts stipulate what will happen if the service becomes unavailable due to an Information Security breach?

- Investigate the Information Security policies and practices of your service providers, partners, customers, and any other parties to which you would be vulnerable in the case of a security breach.

Key #3

Proper Delegation of Program Roles and Components

Responsibility for the Information Management programs must be delegated only to those individuals with appropriate training, qualifications, and authority.

Key Overview

The first two Keys established the roles that clear, consistent rules and guidelines and strong, visible executive leadership play in IMC. Every employee in an organization shares responsibility for compliance, but specific roles and responsibilities also must be created, and appropriate authority delegated to oversee specific program components.

This section explores the importance of properly delegating responsibility for IMC, and provides guidelines to help organizations build an Information Management organizational structure that will promote business interests and protect legal needs.

This section also provides a model organizational structure that you can use to evaluate your organization's current approach.

Chapter 13:

Create an Organizational Structure to Support IMC

In this chapter, we will look at several strategies for delegating authority for Information Management and creating a personnel structure designed to ensure compliance. This is critical because improper delegation not only increases the likelihood that Information Management mistakes will be made, but also can create serious liability for the company. In the next chapter we will look at an actual example of an Information Management organizational structure that you can use to evaluate your current approach.

IMC relies upon an organizational structure to ensure that people with suitable skills, training, experience, and authority are put in charge of IMC in different areas, and at different levels, of the organization. This is not an easy task, and many organizations have struggled to build an Information Management infrastructure that reflects the ongoing transition to electronic business processes, new laws and regulations, and changing business practices in general.

Organizations must have a clearly mapped-out and articulated organizational structure for their Information Management program. Remember that Information Management is a permanent part of your organization's activities, so your organization should have a permanent infrastructure of committees and individuals with assigned Information Management responsibilities.

Specialization Is the Reality

So many issues in the Information Management world increasingly require the participation and advice of specialists. The organizational structure of many companies already reflects this specialization through the creation of executive-level offices such as the Chief Privacy Officer and Chief Security Officer, to name two.

The shifting landscape of privacy law means that developing and implementing a privacy policy increasingly requires the participation of a privacy lawyer or consultant. Decisions need to be made, for example, about which jurisdiction's laws to consider.

Even determining if a specific law affects your organization can be challenging. For example, many organizations have required a lawyer's advice to determine IF they are an entity covered by the Health Insurance Portability and Accountability Act, a complex statute dealing with privacy and many other issues in the healthcare industry.

Your Information Management team needs to be broad enough to cover the full range of legal, business, operational, and compliance issues that must be addressed; and deep enough to ensure that each of these issues is addressed comprehensively.

Legal and IT Must Collaborate

Legal and technology professionals increasingly need to work together to meet their organization's Information Management needs.

This means coordinating efforts to find, preserve, and produce information required for investigations, audits, lawsuits, and other formal proceedings—as neither department is likely to be able to successfully do it alone. For example, a technology department on its own may not be able to determine whether a particular e-record is relevant to a legal action, whereas the legal department may not even know that the information (such as a server log file) even exists.

Training and Certification Should Be Standardized

The process used to determine if employees have the right qualifications for the job should be standardized as much as possible, not only because it will increase the likelihood that staff will have the right skills, but also because it will demonstrate a consistent approach to Information Management to the outside world.

In addition to formal programs offered by post-secondary institutions, a variety of organizations in the Information Management world provide certification and professional designation programs that require varying degrees of training and testing. Some of these include:

- CA—Certified Archivist, offered by the Academy of Certified Archivists

- CRM—Certified Records Manager, offered by the Institute of Certified Records Managers

- MIT—Master of Information Technology, offered by AIIM International

Organizations should also consider offering standardized on-the-job training programs for Information Management program staff that establishes a consistent standard throughout the organization.

The courts, for one, often take an interest in the training, qualifications, and responsibilities of employees who testify on behalf of the company.

For example, in the criminal case of *People v. Bovio*,[132] the original conviction largely hinged on the court's decision to admit an electronically generated bank statement into evidence. The bank statement purported to show that, at the time Bovio purchased nearly $8,000 worth of wholesale diesel fuel with a certified check, he knew that he had insufficient funds in his bank account. Shortly after his check for the diesel fuel bounced, Bovio declared bankruptcy.

Generally speaking, it may be necessary, before an electronic record such as a bank statement can be used as evidence, that a party establish the trustworthiness of the computer *systems* and of the *process* used to prepare the record.

In Bovio's appeal, the court stated,

> It must be shown that the computer equipment [used to generate the evidence, namely the bank statement] is standard, that the entries are made in the regular course of business at or reasonably near the time of the happening of the event recorded, and that the sources of information and the method and time of preparation are such as to indicate trustworthiness and justify admission.

In Bovio's original trial, the prosecutor relied on the testimony of an assistant cashier of the bank to establish the trustworthiness of the bank statement. Although the cashier was able to describe generally how a check is processed, her testimony did not establish

> that the method of preparation at the data center indicates trustworthiness

nor that

> the computer program at the data center was standard, unmodified, and operated according to its instructions.

The assistant bank cashier did not have knowledge of how the data center operated. It is unlikely that she had the training to understand the various technologies employed by the data center, much less to convince a court that they were operating correctly. Her testimony was judged to be insufficient to establish trustworthiness, and the appeal court overturned Bovio's conviction for theft by deception and ordered a new trial.

In this case, it was the prosecutor who made the mistake of calling an unqualified witness to testify about the trustworthiness of the bank statement. But the lesson from our point of view is that Information Management in the electronic age calls for specialized expertise. In the paper world context the assistant cashier might have been perfectly suited to attest to the authenticity of a customer's statement, but not in the electronic age. Similarly, the people responsible for Information Management in various areas of your organization must have different (probably more prodigious) skills, knowledge, and training than they did in years past.

"Extraordinarily Poor Judgment" Costs CEO

As explored in detail beginning on page 136, the case of *Danis v. USN Communications*[133] provides excellent insights into what the court considers good practice in the management and delegation of Information Management program roles and responsibilities. In this shareholder class action lawsuit, the judge found the CEO personally responsible for failing to take an active role in the company's record retention program, and fined him $10,000.

Specifically, the court stated that the CEO "was at fault for delegating" responsibility for preserving company records "to a person who lacked the experience to perform that job properly." The person in question was an in-house attorney with no litigation experience or experience in developing a retention program. The courts also said that the CEO "exhibited extraordinarily poor judgment" by delegating these responsibilities to the attorney, even though he had the option of using the company's outside law firm with deep experience in the area.

Competing Needs: Why Your Committees Need to Be Broad and Deep

Consider this scenario: A manufacturing company deletes all email messages older than 60 days, unless employees have moved them from their inbox to a shared or local hard drive.

However, the Sales Department announces that it wants to keep every email message ever sent between the company and its customers. They even want to duplicate every message and keep one copy in the company's CRM system—forever—because they say the email messages provide invaluable information about customers' buying habits, and enable them to create more accurate sales forecasts. Customer Support agrees, and says that they can use the email archive to create a "living library" of common customer complaints, frequently asked questions, and so on. They claim that customer support costs will drop as a result.

IT/IS isn't happy. They say the extra storage space will cost the company tens of thousands of dollars in extra hardware, maintenance, and staffing costs each year. Frankly, they think keeping email for even 60 days is unnecessary, and would like to see it "blown away" after 30. They also want someone to do something about staff clogging up shared network drives with their personal email treasure troves.

Legal tends to agree with IT. The company's closest competitor has just come through a devastating lawsuit where damaging emails revealed that the company's engineers were aware of a potentially life-threatening flaw in the company's product. A multi-million dollar settlement ensued, their share price plummeted, and this competitor had to lay off employees. Although not unhappy about the competitor's fate, the head of Legal has been lying awake many nights since, wondering what horrors would be revealed in her company's own archives. She wouldn't mind if email messages disappeared as soon as they were read, or better yet, that everyone just went back to using the telephone. For his part, the Records Manager thinks there must be a more disciplined approach to retaining email that supports both business and legal needs.

Will Sales and Customer Support get their wish? Who should make that decision, and whose interests deserve top priority? Even though committees suffer from a reputation as being slow-moving, bureaucratic, and sleep-inducing, they may be the best answer here. Absent a highly-placed, highly-educated, multi-disciplinary executive with too much time on his or her hands, it is unlikely that a single individual can, or even should, make the decision about what is best for the company in this type of situation.

Each stakeholder in this example has a compelling argument.

The company clearly needs to find a solution that balances all departments' needs, one that promotes business needs while protecting legal interests. The only way this solution will be found is through a committee or council where the various stakeholders can communicate their needs and fears, and then work out a solution.

Perhaps the solution is in collecting only the essential information from customer emails and entering it into the CRM system to make

Sales and Customer Service happy, then deleting the emails once they are no longer needed for legal or other purposes to make Legal and IT/IS happy. Perhaps there are technological solutions that can help the company retain email based on content.

Whatever the case, the right solution depends on clear communications amongst all the stakeholders.

Who Should Be Responsible?

As technology, laws, and the business environment continue to evolve; there is undoubtedly confusion in many organizations about what department or individual should be responsible for specific aspects of IMC. Who should spearhead the effort? Is it better to have a senior executive or the resident subject matter expert (e.g., a lawyer, technology professional, Records Management specialist) communicate with the company about IMC policies and procedures?

A 2002 survey of large U.S. industrial companies completed by ARMA International found a great deal of variance amongst organizations in structuring Information and Records Management programs. For example, although most organizations in the survey placed Information and Records Management responsibility within one of two departments (business services or legal), the survey found 11 other departments were also used.[134]

Answer the following questions to illustrate some of the issues in this area that may seem subtle, but nonetheless can have an enormous effect on the success of your Information Management program.

> 1) A health insurer assembles a committee to deal with HIPAA. On the eve of disseminating the new company privacy policy via email, the company decides to place the name of the committee in the "from" field of the email and at the top of the policy itself, to give credit to all who participated. Do you think having the committee's name on the email, rather than the CIO's name, is the best way to get attention of all 40,000 employees?
>
> 2) The Knowledge Management Director sends out a memo to the various Business Unit Heads seeking their participation

in a new databases sharing initiative, which would enable cross-selling to customers. Was she the right person to carry the banner for the new company project?

3) A Records Analyst contacts the Information Security Director seeking help in gathering information requested in a subpoena from a regulator. He figures that the head of Information Security would be the right place to start. Is he right?

While the right answers to these questions depends on a number of factors, including the unique nature of each organization, the questions illustrate the challenges that organizations face when deciding who should be responsible for Information Management program elements.

While the committee members in the first question clearly understand the issues at hand, they may not be the best choice to carry the new policy banner forward. Important changes like this require the visibility that only high-level executive involvement can typically provide.

In the second question, the head of a department designed to serve the needs of the Business Units is not likely to have the authority or visibility to compel the Business Unit heads to expend time and energy on a project that does not have the blessing of corporate executives.

Finally, in the third question, although the Information Security Director clearly may have a role to play in helping the company gather information responsive to the subpoena, there are complex legal issues at play that must be addressed and managed by the company's legal department.

Delegation May Be There, Even If It's Not On Paper

In *United States v. Van Riper*,[135] a gas station company was convicted of violating several regulations because of the acts of one of its managers. The company argued that only the manager, and not the company, should be held accountable for the violations. The company argued that the company "bore no responsibility" for the acts of the manager, as his illegal acts were not "within the scope of his authority."

However, the court found that the head of the company had "in effect delegated... full authority to conduct that gas station," to the manager, so his illegal acts were within the scope of his responsibilities. As such, the company itself could be charged with the manager's violations.

The court went on to say:

If [a manager] caused the corporation to violate the law, then the corporation can be held liable even though the officers and directors of the corporation were ignorant of what actually was done... Otherwise a corporation could escape criminal liability by the simple expedient of the persons responsible for its corporate existence and management failing to perform the functions imposed upon them by corporation law.

In other words, organizations have a duty to supervise the activities of employees to whom they delegate authority, and to ensure that those employees can adequately do their job.

Chapter 14:

A Sample Information Management Organizational Structure

Although the number of possible ways to create an Information Management organizational structure is probably the same as the number of different organizations doing business, there are some basic concepts that all organizations can use.

This chapter presents one possible model for an Information Management organizational structure. It is based on models used by many large institutions across the country. Its specific makeup and components will vary by organization, depending on size and other factors, but the basic elements and approach should help all organizations evaluate their approach to Information Management.

About This Model

This model Information Management organizational structure is designed for a large company with a central corporate entity and several business units that operate with varying degrees of independence from the corporate entity. Both the corporate office and the business units are further divided into departments. Smaller organizations also need to ensure that they have an organizational structure appropriate to ensure IMC, even though they may not have the human or financial resources to adopt a model with the scale of the one outlined here.

The model structure is designed to be implemented by a central corporate entity, which then "distributes" the structure to the various units in such a way that there is consistency across the entire organization, yet enough flexibility for "special cases" to be dealt with appropriately. For example, the various committees and councils across the entire organization use a consistent naming convention, which helps to clarify that their mandates are the same, no matter where they reside within the organization. On the flexibility side, however, individual business units have the ability to create special committees to address issues unique to their unit but not easily addressed by the "central" committees' staff by the corporate Information Management Department.

The model has two basic parts. First, it identifies the various committees and councils that comprise the organizational structure, and explains their roles and responsibilities. This first part of the model is written in a formal manner as you might find it in an Information Management manual or similar policy.

The model's second part describes the various individual roles that designated staff members play in the Information Management program.

The Councils

The Executive Information Management Council is at the top of the Information Management organizational structure. Executives from the various stakeholder departments throughout the corporation populate this Council.

The stakeholder organizations in this example are:

- Legal

- Human Resources

- Information Technology/Information Systems

- Finance

- Records Management

- Business Risk Management

- Tax and Audit

- Compliance

- Affected Business Units

Although you may not have all of these departments in your organization, or they may have different names, this list illustrates the need to form a group that is large enough to encompass an appropriate range of business functions without being unwieldy.

The Information Management Committees

The Council has the ability to create multi-disciplinary committees at the corporate level. Since corporate-level committees address high-level issues, they must be broadly based. High-level issues may include, for example:

- Privacy

- Sarbanes-Oxley

- Records Retention

- Records Preservation

- Electronic Records

This basic structure of a high-level council and subordinate committees (some of which will be addressed in this section) is duplicated at each business unit, with the only difference being that representatives come from the related business unit, and their primary focus is limited to Information Management issues within their unit only.

Individual Roles and Responsibilities

As explored in the previous chapter, organizations must assign specific Information Management responsibilities to qualified and experienced people, including the following:

- **Information Management Director.** A corporate executive with oversight of the organization-wide Information Management program.

- **Information Management Managers.** Business unit-level managers with responsibility for the Information Management program within their business unit.

- **Information Management Coordinators.** Department-level, "on-the-ground" experts with day-to-day responsibility for the Information Management program in their department.

- **Responsible Attorney.** The corporate attorney responsible for issuing Records Hold Orders.

The Model

The following model is for informational purposes only. Seek the advice of counsel before adopting any such organizational model.

A. Executive Information Management Council

The Executive Information Management Council ("Council") shall have company-wide responsibility for ensuring that the Information Management Program is implemented throughout the company. It shall also ensure that Information Management policies and procedures are in place to address operational, legal, and technical needs and requirements.

The Council shall meet periodically and shall be coordinated by the Information Management Department. The Council shall be comprised of representatives from the Legal, Human Resources, Information Technology, Finance, Information Management, Business Risk Management, Tax and Audit, and Compliance departments. Specific activities of the Council and its Committees shall include, but not be limited to, assisting in the reviewing and approving of Policy, Retention Rules, storage practices, implementation of the various aspects of the Information Management Program, and development of new policies, rules, or directives regarding records, as needed.

The Executive Information Management Council shall create and oversee the Committees outlined below. The Council may create additional Committees as required.

Executive Records Retention Committee

The Executive Records Retention Committee ("Retention Committee") shall be responsible for drafting, reviewing, approving, and implementing the company-wide Retention Rules. The Retention Committee shall be comprised of representatives from the Information Management, Legal, and Compliance departments, at a minimum. Specific activities shall include, but not be limited to, soliciting feedback and approval from the heads of affected Business Units when the Retention Rules are updated, and approving any records disposition.

Executive Records Preservation Committee

The Executive Records Preservation Committee ("Preservation Committee") shall be responsible for drafting, reviewing, approving, and implementing policies and procedures related to the preservation of electronic or paper records required for threatened or current audits, investigations, and/or litigation. The Preservation Committee shall be comprised of representatives from the Information Management, Legal, Tax and Audit, and Information Technology departments, at a minimum. The Preservation Committee's activities shall include, but not be limited to, creating and implementing a process for the issuance, management, and termination of Records Hold Orders.

Executive Electronic Records Committee

The Executive Electronic Records Committee ("E-Records Committee") shall be responsible for drafting, reviewing, approving, and implementing policies and procedures relating to the management of electronic records. The E-Records Committee shall be comprised of representatives from the Information Management and Information Technology departments, at a minimum. Specific activities shall include, but not be limited to, addressing any electronic records issues and developing policies and procedures relating to electronic records.

B. Business Unit Information Management Council

Each Business Unit, under the direction of the Executive Information Management Council and the Information Management department, shall develop a Business Unit Information Management Council, which shall be responsible for activities similar to those undertaken by the Executive Information Management Council, with the functional difference being the limitation of scope to their specific Business Unit. Business Unit Information Management Councils and Committees shall be comprised of Business Unit representatives from the same departments as those comprising the Executive Records Councils and Committees. In addition to addressing the issues of Records Retention, Records Holds, and Electronic Records, each Business Unit Information Management Council and its Committees may also address additional or different Information Management-related issues impacting their Business Unit.

Each Business Unit Information Management Council shall create and oversee the Committees outlined below. Each Council may create additional Committees as required.

Business Unit Records Retention Committee

The Business Unit Records Retention Committee ("Retention Committee") shall be responsible for working with the Executive Records Retention Committee to ensure that the Retention Schedule (and other retention-related policies and procedures) meet the Business Unit's legal, operational, and technical requirements. The Retention Committee shall also be responsible for ensuring that the Retention Schedule is fully implemented and adhered to throughout the Business Unit. The Retention Committee shall also sign off on any records disposition within their Business Unit.

Business Unit Records Preservation Committee

The Business Unit Records Preservation Committee ("Preservation Committee") shall be responsible for assisting the Executive Records Preservation Committee with the implementation of the Records Hold

Policy and other Records Hold-related procedures and notification mechanisms. The Preservation Committee shall help to ensure that their Business Unit meets its ongoing responsibilities for records preservation related to specific Records Hold Orders (including Litigation and Tax Holds). The Preservation Committee may undertake training of employees on records preservation issues within their Business Unit.

Business Unit Electronic Records Committee

The Business Unit Electronic Records Committee ("E-Records Committee") shall be responsible for assisting the Executive Electronic Records Committee by reviewing and implementing any policies and procedures specifically required to address the proper management of electronic records within their Business Unit. The E-Records Committee may undertake additional or different Electronic Records issues within their Business Unit.

C. Individual Roles and Responsibilities

Information Management Director

The Information Management Director shall have high-level primary responsibility for architecting and implementing the Information Management Program. All policies, rules, and procedures affecting records shall involve the Information Management Director. The Information Management Director shall have primary responsibility for:

- Developing and implementing the Information Management Program;

- Implementing the retention schedule;

- Managing the offsite storage vendor relationship;

- Assisting with Councils and Committees at the Executive and Business Unit levels;

- Assisting with implementation of the Records Hold process; and,

- Training and oversight of Business Unit Information Management Managers.

Business Unit Information Management Managers

Each Business Unit shall appoint one or more Information Management Managers with responsibility for one or more departments within their Business Unit. Information Management Manager responsibilities shall include, but not be limited to:

- Administration of the Information Management Program within the Business Unit;

- Conducting Business Unit records training;

- Monitoring Business Unit compliance with the Information Management Program;

- Managing the proper disposition of records;

- Managing the implementation of Records Holds and the general preservation of required records;

- Serving on their Business Unit Information Management Council;

- Managing Business Unit preservation and retention of all types of records, regardless of format or media (i.e., electronic, film-based, and paper records); and,

- Training and oversight of Information Management Coordinators.

Information Management Coordinators

Each Business Unit shall appoint one or more Information Management Coordinators with responsibility for one or more departments within their Business Unit. Information Management Coordinator responsibilities shall include, but not be limited to:

- Assisting with the implementation of, and compliance with, the Information Management Program and any records-related policies and procedures affecting their respective department(s);

- Helping to ensure compliance with the Retention Schedule, and implementing changes to the Retention Schedule;

- Overseeing daily operations relating to inactive records;

- Assisting in moving inactive records to offsite storage;

- Communicating and coordinating with offsite storage vendors;

- Assisting departmental employees with records-related issues and questions;

- Assisting with the disposition of records; and,

- Assisting with the implementation of Records Holds and general preservation of required records.

Responsible Attorney

The Responsible Attorney shall be responsible for the implementation of Records Hold Orders for threatened and/or current audits, investigations, and/or litigation requiring the preservation of records and other potential evidence in the company's possession, care, custody, or control. Other responsibilities shall include, but not be limited to:

- Disseminating the Records Hold information to all relevant employees, Information Management Managers, Business Unit heads, and the Information Management Department;

- Determining what records and other materials are covered by a Records Hold, and so advising employees in a manner that provides sufficient notice and understanding about what actions employees need to take to preserve and produce records;

- Working with Information Management Coordinators and Information Technology staff to ensure that electronic records covered by a Records Hold are preserved;

- Periodically reviewing Records Holds in effect to ensure that preservation is still required; and,

- Issuing a Notice of Termination of a Records Hold when the relevant audit, investigation, or litigation has concluded.

©2004, Randolph A. Kahn, ESQ., and Barclay T. Blair. For informational purposes only. Seek the advice of counsel before adopting any such organizational model.

Key #4

Program Communication and Training

The organization must take steps to effectively communicate Information Management policies and procedures to all employees. These steps might include, for example, requiring all employees to participate in training programs, and the dissemination of information that explains in a practical and understandable manner what is expected of employees.

Key Overview

Once your organization's leadership supports and promotes your Information Management policies and procedures, the Information Management organizational structure is in place, and the right policies and procedures have been created, the organization must take steps to effectively communicate the policies and procedures to all employees.

Chapter 15:

Essential Elements of Information Management Communication and Training

Case after case has demonstrated that, whether they like or not, companies and government agencies can be held accountable for their failure to adequately train and monitor their employees' actions. IMC depends upon a comprehensive and consistent ongoing program of communication and training. Organizations cannot expect their managers and staff to comply with Information Management directives unless they are given the guidance and training that they need.

Be Clear and Consistent

It was recently reported that a happy eBay bidder purchased a used Blackberry, a mobile email device that normally sells for hundreds of dollars new, for less than $20.[136] The seller was a former VP at a major investment bank who had left the firm months earlier and no longer needed the device.

When the buyer powered up the BlackBerry, he found that it contained a wealth of information, including:

- About 200 internal company emails that revealed information such as loan terms for various investment bank customers, non-public information about mergers and restructuring, and discussions with a customer about whether or not they should strictly adhere to the terms of contract.

- A database containing the contact information (in some cases, even home phone numbers) of more than 1,000 of the bank's employees, including senior executives.

- Personal email messages revealing the VP's brokerage account numbers and mortgage payment amounts.

In this case, the company and the VP got very lucky, because the buyer was a "good guy" who reported his find. However, the potential implications of the information getting into the wrong hands are staggering, and can include:

- **Contract and privacy violations.** Violations of customer contracts, and privacy and confidentiality agreements.

- **Espionage.** Loss of trade secrets and business intelligence to competitors.

- **HR.** Loss of key executives to headhunters armed with personnel information.

- **Regulatory.** Violations of securities laws concerning the release of non-public information affecting public companies.

- **Internal policies.** Violation of internal data protection policies, employee privacy policies, and other policies and procedures.

How Did This Happen?

The cause of this near disaster seems to have been a combination of a lack of training and inconsistent policy enforcement.

For his part, the VP allegedly thought that by removing the battery, all information on the device would be erased, although the device's memory does not require battery power to function. He also thought that when the bank (his former employer) terminated his email account on the day he left the company, email records residing on the device would also be deleted, which is not how the technology works. Rather, data can only be erased manually by using the device's syncing software, or remotely through a command from a properly configured server. The VP simply had not been trained regarding the compliance aspects of his device.

As for policy enforcement, the bank did have a policy that requires employees to return any mobile devices belonging to the firm before they leave the company. Simple enough, but in this case, the device did not belong to the firm—it was purchased by the VP using his own money, and then configured to access the firm's email system by the bank's IT department. It that case, the company says that their policy requires a departing employee to hand the device in for erasure before they leave—a policy that clearly was not enforced in this case.

There are any number of reasons why the policy was not enforced. Perhaps an HR employee was reluctant to demand that a senior executive hand over his BlackBerry. Perhaps the HR employee was not aware of the policy. Perhaps they both believed that removing batteries was enough.

Whatever the case, organizations need to ensure that sensitive information is adequately protected, regardless of where it resides. This is done through promoting awareness of the capabilities and Information Management implications of the technology employed throughout the organizations, ensuring that policies and procedures reflect those capabilities, and finally, ensuring that those policies are enforced consistently, regardless of how awkward or sensitive that may be.

Clarity Is King

In Key 1, Chapter 7, we talked about the need to create policies and procedures that are clear and unambiguous. However, this careful work will be undone if communication and training related to the policy is unclear. This was clearly illustrated in *Garrity v. John Hancock Mut. Life Ins. Co.*,[137] where two female employees were terminated because they violated the company's email policy that prohibited "messages that are defamatory, abusive, obscene, profane, sexually oriented, threatening, or racially offensive."[138]

The policy also expressed very clearly that the company reserved the right to review and inspect email sent or received on the corporate email system.

Despite these policy elements, when a fellow employee complained about sexually explicit email being sent and received over the corporate email system, and the company reviewed the offending email messages, the plaintiffs claimed that their privacy had been violated. Among other things, in their wrongful termination and defamation suit against Hancock, they asserted that the employer had violated their privacy because it "had led them to believe that these personal emails could be kept private with the use of personal passwords and email folders."

So despite the fact that the employer had written clear policies regarding email privacy and the company's right to review employees' email, it had also sent mixed messages to employees. Perhaps by allowing employees to create folders specifically for personal emails, protected by different passwords, they created the impression that—policy notwithstanding—those email messages would be private.

Organizations need to be careful to be clear and consistent—not only in the language of policies and procedures, but also in the way they communicate with employees about all Information Management issues.

Be Concise

Disseminate to your employees only those policies and procedures that they need to fulfill their Information Management obligations. You may also need to provide supplementary information that explains or supports the Information Management policies and procedures and you may even want to give employees related but non-essential information that they might find useful or interesting, as long as it is concise and focused.

But do not overwhelm employees with extraneous or excessive information—that only sends a message that you do not value their time and haven't done your homework, and increases the likelihood that the information (even that which is on point) will be ignored altogether.

In our consulting practice we have seen too many companies include information about firewalls and security administration, for example, in Records Management manuals. The procedures for properly configuring a company firewall, though undoubtedly full of amazing intrigue and plot twists, are completely useless to an administrative assistant, or a CEO for that matter. The same goes for intricate procedures dealing with offsite storage vendors in companies where only Records Management staff ever have dealings with those vendors; and so on.

Unnecessary information like this works against good Information Management program communication and training, not for it.

Be Visible

All executives, managers, and staff with designated responsibilities for Information Management program components must offer consistent and visible support for the program. In addition, the policy and procedure communications to employees must be consistent, regardless of where they are situated within the organization.

As explored earlier in the Leadership section, it is critical that top executives demonstrate their support for the Information Management program by communicating its importance directly to employees. This can be done through email messages, voicemail blasts, face-to-face presentations, teleconferences, and many other ways as appropriate, depending on the size and culture of the organization. Regardless of the method used, it is important that the communications are consistent with the messages provided elsewhere by the program's policies and procedures.

This leadership message must then be carried forward by every level of the Information Management and Records Management team as they manage, coordinate, and implement the program.

It is also important that those responsible for day-to-day Information Management tasks are visible and approachable. Each employee needs to know who is responsible for answering questions, supervising, and assisting them with the Information Management task in their area, and know how to reach them. One way to ensure that this happens is by fostering an environment of "customer service" amongst technology personnel responsible for Information Management—for example, by measuring performance and compensating them on this aspect of their jobs.

Be Proactive and Responsive

It is critical that organizations are proactive in communicating Information Management program elements to all employees in a timely fashion. This means that organizations must:

- Address problems as soon as they arise

- Anticipate problems that may arise in the future and take steps to address them now

This is especially the case when employees have information in their possession that needs to be preserved because it is relevant to potential or current litigation.

For example, In *Testa v. Wal-Mart Stores*,[139] a truck driver successfully sued Wal-Mart for negligence because he slipped on an icy loading dock while making a delivery of tropical fish to a Wal-Mart store.

Wal-Mart appealed, claiming that the dock was icy because it was not accepting deliveries that day due to a grand opening celebration. The vendors, including Mr. Testa, were told not to make deliveries. Therefore, Wal-Mart had not cleared the loading dock. Wal-Mart further claimed that, despite having been informed that Wal-Mart was not accepting deliveries on that day, Testa still made the delivery; and Wal-Mart warehouse staff felt obliged to receive the order of tropical fish.

However, in the case, Wal-Mart was unable to produce purchase orders or telephone records supporting its claim that it had warned Testa. An invoice clerk had disposed of these records before the trial began, "pursuant to a standard record-retention policy." The invoice clerk testified that "she did not know about the accident at the time and no one instructed her to preserve either the purchase order or the telephone records."

The court makes clear that it may assume that the contents of documents destroyed by a party, when they know that the documents may *potentially* be relevant to current or *potential* litigation, were in fact "unfavorable to that party." As the court clarifies, this idea

> springs from the commonsense notion that a party who

destroys a document (or permits it to be destroyed) when facing litigation, knowing the document's relevancy to issues in the case, may well do so out of a sense that the document's contents hurt his position.

The court found that Wal-Mart had failed to inform the invoice clerk about the need to preserve records relevant to the accident. Wal-Mart had conducted an internal accident investigation immediately after the incident, and had also produced a report noting that it was likely that Testa would sue.

Moreover, the court states that the most relevant issue when determining what the consequences of improper document destruction (spoliation) should be is not the specific knowledge of the employee who destroyed the record:

> [T]he critical part... depends, rather, on institutional notice— the aggregate knowledge possessed by a party and its agents, servants, and employees.

In other words, since Wal-Mart knew about the accident and the likelihood of ensuing litigation, it had an obligation to inform all employees of the need to preserve information potentially relevant to that litigation. A jury is free to interpret a company's failure to provide this notification, and thereby allowing evidence to be destroyed, as an indication that the contents of the destroyed documents would have been damaging to the company's case.

This case illustrates the need for organizations to be proactive when dealing with all Information Management scenarios where they have a reasonable expectation that records may be needed in the event of a dispute or regulatory matter.

Offer Engaging and Interactive Training Programs

There is no excuse in today's technology-rich environment for offering static, dreary Information Management training programs that neither engage nor effectively educate the trainee. Aside from specialist computer programs designed for large companies with multiple training programs and thousands of employees, even the smallest company can inexpensively use a bit of Web programming and a small intranet to bring employees interactive and engaging training programs to help to bring the concepts of the Information Management program to life.

Intranet-Based

An organization's internal website, or intranet, can be a valuable resource in disseminating the information and training that employees need to comply with the Information Management program. An intranet can not only be used to provide directed training that includes video and other multimedia elements, but it can also provide a library of supplementary reference materials that employees may need as they are faced with various Information Management challenges.

For example, an intranet can be a great tool for providing information on Records or Legal Holds. This is not information that every employee needs every day, but when a group of employees are affected by potential or ongoing litigation, a pre-built library of focused information about their specific responsibilities will be invaluable.

In addition, the intranet can be used to provide timely updates and notifications regarding Records Holds and other urgent Information Management topics by providing links to the content in email messages broadcast to the employees.

Instructor-Led Training

Even with advances in training technology that offer an array of interactive and entertaining elements for self-directed training, for many trainees there is no substitute for the human element. An experienced instructor can tailor his or her material "on the fly" to meet the needs of the group being trained, and can be much more responsive to questions and problems (as well as add humor and other engaging elements that are hard to duplicate in the self-directed environment).

Choosing to use instructor-led training over online or other forms of training can also send a message to employees about the relative importance of the topic. For example, bringing in outside instructors to talk about the importance of the Records Hold process is likely to create a stronger impression on most employees than an email message from their manager containing a URL for yet another round of Web-based training on the topic. Many organizations have used this approach in the past when their companies have been damaged by improper Information Management practices.

While face-to-face instructor-led training may not always be practical for large organizations with thousands of employees spread across the globe, many of the same benefits can still be offered by remote instructor-led training sessions that use video conferencing and interactive training materials.

Make IMC an Employee Priority

While organizations may hope that each employee cares about the Information Management program simply because they are all highly ethical, motivated people who wish to act in the company's best interests, such thinking has unfortunately gotten too many organizations in trouble. While most employees in any given organization undoubtedly want to do the right thing, it is not that majority which causes the majority of the problems. In any case, it is not the ethical or responsible thing for the leaders of any organizations to blindly hope that employees will educate themselves and comply with the Information Management program just because they are nice people.

Rather, employees need incentives to comply. In other words, give them a reason to care about the Information Management program by making clear to them that their compliance is an important aspect of their job, their compliance will be measured, and their compensation will be based in part on their compliance (the carrot). Also, make clear that a failure to comply will not be tolerated and may result in discipline, including termination and legal action (the stick).

Perhaps the most important—and most overlooked—aspect of encouraging employee compliance, however, is that *employees must be provided with the time and opportunity to fulfill their Information Management responsibilities and participate in the training programs.* Consider this example. A recent survey conducted by AIIM

International and Kahn Consulting, Inc.[140] found that 65% of email users spend at least a quarter of their working day writing, reading, and managing email, and 25% of users spend more than half of their working day on those tasks.

Imagine a company where the majority of employees are spending a quarter of their time just coping with the daily email flood. The company is just coming out of a lawsuit where several "smoking gun" email messages were found in the email archive which were very painful and damaging to the company—causing them to lose the case and a raft of customers too. So, the company has decided to change the way it manages email. From now on employees will "manage it by content." The company has created a new Retention Schedule that identifies 75 different categories of records that they expect to find in email and have provided this list of categories to the employees as part of a half-hour training session. At the session, the employees also learned that from now on they must manually select one of these 75 categories from a pop-up list in their email program *for every email message they send or receive*. The employees are told that this new "email coding" process will help the company meet its legal obligations.

How much extra time do you think this new process will take each employee, each day? Another 5%, or 10% on top of the 25% of the day they already spend managing their email?

Management has two choices. They can reduce employees' workload to provide more time to do their email coding chores, and be realistic about how this change will affect employee productivity—and adjust their forecasts and expectations to match. Or they can make no realistic adjustment to their employees' workload, and have employees failing to complete projects on time, working longer hours, and generally suffering from lower morale. In the latter scenario, many employees will learn to cope in the way that is least likely to affect their performance: by hastily and improperly coding email messages, thereby putting the company right back where it started with improperly managed email records.

Too many organizations today are guilty of making the latter choice, and failing to give employees the tools (or time) they need to comply with critical Information Management policies and procedures. Without the tools, employees lose their motivation. Of course, the tools also need to be used and configured properly. In this case, the company should also investigate less time-consuming ways to properly code email, by compressing the list of email categories, and configuring the technology so that employees only see a customized list of categories that apply to their work.

Constantly Communicate and Train

Communicating with employees about the Information Management program is an ongoing process that should be a continuous part of an organization's culture and day-to-day operations. Although employees can learn Information Management fundamentals through one-time training sessions, ongoing reminders and refreshers will also be necessary. There are number of reasons why training must be continuous, as explored below.

1. Keep Current With the Latest Laws and Regulations

As explored in detail in Key 1 on page 77, an organization must keep its Information Management policies and procedures current with changes in the law and regulatory environment. This requires periodic review and updating of not only the core policies and procedures, but also the communications and training materials used to support them.

For example, *Email Policies and Practices: An Industry Study Conducted by AIIM International and Kahn Consulting, Inc.*, found that a majority of organizations are making or plan to make changes to the way they manage email as a result of Sarbanes-Oxley and recent high-profile business failures, litigation, and corporate malfeasance. About 68% of those organizations plan to create new policies. New or updated policies addressing email management have a direct bearing on all employees using the email system, so these organizations will need to communicate the changes and update related training materials.

Policy and procedure revisions should be communicated in a professional and formal manner to those employees affected by the changes.

2. Adjust to Major Events

Organizations also need to communicate with the employees when major events have a real or potential impact on the Information Management program. Events that should trigger communication from senior executives, managers, and/or Records Management staff include the following:

- **Mergers, acquisitions, and other major changes to the way the organization operates.** These upheavals often result in a change of culture, changes in the hierarchy of Information Management responsibility and authority, revisions of policies and procedures, new technology or reconfigurations of existing technology, turnover of committee membership, and so on.

- **New executives.** Changes in leadership may have a direct impact on who is responsible for Information Management and how the program is managed.

- **Changes in Information Management organizational structure.** Major changes to the Information Management organizational structure, such as the creation of new committees or roles, and the retirement of temporary committees or roles.

- **Terminations and other public disciplinary actions related to Information Management.** The mass firing of 40 employees for violating the company Internet use policy, theft of company information, or unauthorized use of unlicensed software undoubtedly requires authorization from an organization's leaders. However, less spectacular, localized disciplinary actions, legal action, and termination can possibly be handled by department managers' HR representatives.

- **Litigation.** Lawsuits can precipitate an atmosphere of crisis, and senior executives must communicate with the organization to reassure employees and especially ensure that those who may have information in their care, custody, or control that is potentially relevant to litigation know exactly what to do.

3. Educate Employees about the Implication of New Technology

Changes in an organization's technology environment that affect employee's Information Management responsibilities should trigger new communication and perhaps training. For example, the adoption of desktop email encryption technology would likely require updates to existing email policies and training materials that explain to employees how to use the technology to encrypt the email before they send it.

New technology can be exciting for employees, but it can also be a burden—just one more thing that they need to learn. So it behooves organizations to give the employees adequate training and support. Failure to do so could result not only in diminished productivity, but also serious liability, as illustrated by the BlackBerry device example provided at the beginning of this chapter.

New or updated technology may require employee communication and training on a host of issues, including:

- **How to use new applications securely.** Even the smallest mistakes can create big headaches for companies, such as employees opening email attachments that contain viruses, or downloading "free" software from the Internet that contains keylogging "spyware." Employees need to be trained on the security do's and don'ts of new technology before it is deployed.

- **Appropriate uses of new technology.** Just because a piece of software or hardware can accomplish a particular task doesn't mean that it should be used in that way. For example, an employer-supplied PDA may be able to send and receive an employee's personal email, but that does not mean that the company should allow it to be used in that way. The intermingling of work and personal email may create a range of privacy and professional issues that the company should avoid by providing a new acceptable-use policy that prohibits the practice—especially if the IT/IS department cannot prevent it through configuration controls.

- **Employee responsibilities.** Employees must clearly understand exactly what their responsibilities are in regards to new technology. For example, are they responsible for capturing their Instant Messaging conversations with customers and storing them somewhere, or does the software do it automatically?

- **Managing output.** Each new technology will likely generate information that must be managed. It is the company's responsibility to have rules in place before the technology is implemented, to ensure from the very beginning that information is properly managed.

Key #5

Auditing and Monitoring to Measure Program Compliance

The organization must take reasonable steps to measure compliance with Information Management policies and procedures by utilizing monitoring and auditing programs.

Key Overview

The best Information Management policies and practices in the world will not protect an organization unless they have the means to find out if employees are in fact complying with those directives. This is the role of auditing and monitoring—to provide management with a method of measuring and improving IMC.

Chapter 16:

Use Auditing and Monitoring to Measure IMC

An organization's work is not complete, even after it has drafted policies and has trained employees. Rather, organizations need to continue their commitment to IMC by establishing programs to audit and monitor compliance with the Information Management program.

Information Management Auditing and Monitoring

Auditing in the financial world is, of course, a formal discipline practiced by highly trained auditing specialists. The term "audit" as used in this book has a more general meaning that includes any practice designed to *periodically measure and report on compliance with a set of standards or criteria.* In this sense, "auditing" activities in the Information Management world are often referred to in many other ways, such as assessment, evaluation, review, survey, validation, and so on. Although these terms all have specific, formal meanings in a variety of financial, technical, regulatory, and operational environments, the focus of this section is not on differentiating amongst these activities, but to explore how their concepts can be used to help organizations increase IMC.

Monitoring is a related, but separate concept. The goal of monitoring is generally the same as auditing, except that it is performed on an *ongoing* basis. So, Information Management monitoring is the *ongoing measurement and reporting on compliance with a set of standards or criteria.* In other words, Information Management auditing and monitoring are both designed to find out exactly what is happening in an organization, but auditing accomplishes this by looking at the past, whereas monitoring accomplishes this by looking at what is happening right now.

Together, Information Management auditing and monitoring provide a two-pronged management control that is essential for ensuring that an organization is meeting its Information Management goals and obligations.

Find Out before Someone Else Does

Putting it simply, Information Management auditing and monitoring matter because, as the saying goes, "If you can't measure, you can't manage it." Auditing and monitoring allow organizations to understand where their Information Management program is succeeding and where it is failing, and correct any compliance problems before they blossom into full-fledged disasters. In other words, auditing and monitoring allow you to find out about your problems before someone else—like a court, regulator, auditor, or shareholder.

A few years ago our consulting firm was engaged to perform an audit of a large client's imaging system that used two parallel, identical, high-volume document scanners. During the audit we found that, although the scanners were identical, one had incorrectly been set up to scan documents at nearly half the resolution of the other. This configuration variance had not been discovered by the organization. Even though the client was confident that documents scanned at the lower resolution still adequately captured the information contained in the original paper documents, they had not considered the potential consequences of their configuration inconsistency.

We asked our clients to imagine themselves on the witness stand at trial, being cross-examined about the accuracy of the scanned electronic documents created by their system. We suggested that the exchange might look something like this:

Attorney: So, because one scanner was set at nearly double the resolution, then did it technically capture more information?

Client witness: Yes, well, I suppose…

Attorney: So, is it possible that if a document that had lightly handwritten notes and comments on it, those notes would be picked up by one scanner and not the other?

Client witness: Well, I suppose it is possible, but not likely.

Attorney: So, you are saying that it is in fact possible that an electronic document imaged by the low-resolution scanner may not actually contain all the information of the original document?

Client witness: Well, I guess…

Attorney: Are you aware that a central issue in this case is whether or not your company's electronic records are accurate, and whether or not this court can rely on them?

Client witness: Yes, I was told that, but…

Attorney: And yet, you sit here today and have told us that your system for scanning and imaging electronic records might be inadequate. And that it is possible that all the information found on an original paper records may not actually be captured by the low-resolution scanner, that… (and so on)

What is happening in this exchange is that the attorney is trying to raise doubt in the jury's mind about the company's scanning procedures. The company's own practices and their investment in high-resolution scanners indicated that they thought it was necessary to scan documents at the higher resolution. If the company itself believed that this was necessary, and yet did not do it consistently, how can they expect the jury to not have questions about the accuracy of the scanned records?

Had the company implemented an auditing or monitoring program that used techniques such as routinely comparing the file size or resolution of scanned documents, and so on, this potential litigation issue would not have existed. What seems insignificant today might provide a litigator with ammunition tomorrow.

Auditing and Monitoring Programs Help to Build Trust

Developing and implementing good Information Management policies and procedures demonstrates to employees and to the outside world that the organization takes its Information Management obligations seriously. Developing and carrying out auditing and monitoring programs is the next step in demonstrating this commitment and building trust. These programs demonstrate that not only is the organization willing to spend the time and money required to develop the policies, but also to ensure that employees stay in compliance.

Besides, if you are reluctant to take your Information Management obligations seriously, the courts and regulators might force you to do so.

For example, in the case of *Smith v. Texaco*,[141] the court deemed it necessary to issue a temporary restraining order (TRO) against a Texas oil company that was accused of discrimination. The TRO prevented the company from "moving, altering, or deleting any records which might pertain to Smith's… claims of employment discrimination against" the company.

The court's concern appears to have been justified, because it later found that, "but for Smith's efforts to enforce the TRO," the company would have moved records out of state that were "possibly essential for making Smith's case, and certainly relevant to the claim or the defense."

The Securities and Exchange Commission went one step further during its investigation of WorldCom, imposing an $800-an-hour monitor on the company to ensure that the company did not destroy evidence of its accounting debacle, and that it had "developed document retention policies and… [had] complied with these policies."[142] The monitor was a former chairman of the SEC.

In these two cases, the companies were acting in a manner that apparently created suspicion with the court and the regulator, not trust. Their failure to carrying out adequate auditing and monitoring placed them under increased scrutiny.

Application of Retention Rules to E-Records

If there is any area that could use auditing in today's organizations, it is the proper retention and disposition of electronic records. Auditing in this area can include a range of activities, from complex system inventories, to a review of basic Records Management software configuration and functionality. At a minimum, organizations need to make sure that records are being retained for the proper length of time, whether the records are in paper or electronic form.

This was clearly demonstrated in a complex case in 2000 that dealt with excessive force allegations against the city of Columbus, Ohio police force.[143] A local newspaper requested police records, including complaints against city police officers. The city was required to retain disciplinary records under the state's public records laws, and their retention rules stipulated that the records in question be retained for three years.

Although the paper records had been destroyed in accordance with the retention rules, the city had not destroyed the electronic versions of these records. As a result, disciplinary records dating back almost 10 years were available in electronic form.[144]

A lengthy legal battle ensued over the release of the older records, with the court ultimately deciding that the city's failure to dispose of the records according to their own retention rules did not change the fact that the older records were still records that the public had the right to access. As such, the records were released to the newspaper.

Organizations need to ensure that paper and electronic records are being managed consistently, and that retention rules are followed regardless of where records reside or the medium upon which they are stored.

Know What Is Happening on Your Own Networks

In July 2003, a software company sued a competitor for electronic espionage. The company claimed to have found evidence in the log files of its private File Transfer Protocol (FTP) server that showed that the competitor had been accessing the server over the period of a year. Over the course of the year, the company claimed, more than 900 sensitive files had been accessed and downloaded, including contact information for nearly 110,000 of the company's customers and prospects. The company also claimed that the competitor had downloaded confidential advertising materials and used them to create a nearly identical campaign of its own. According to the company, the competitor was able to gain access to the server by using the confidential username and password of an employee (and also an "anonymous" account), who was not suspected of being involved in the espionage.[145] If the allegations of intellectual property theft and espionage in this case are true, the company clearly had good reason to bring legal action.

Many organizations have found themselves in similar situations where they have suffered losses as a result of security breaches. This case and others like it illustrate the need for all organizations to be prepared to ask hard questions about their ability to monitor and audit activities on their own servers. In this case, questions such as the following should be asked:

- How did the outsider get access to the usernames and passwords of its employees? Was the outsider able to guess the passwords based on the employees' names or other data points? Were the passwords "bad" in that they were easily guessable or default system passwords? Does the company have a password policy and was it enforced?

- Why was the company's customer list and other "crown jewels" protected only by a username and password? To state the obvious, perhaps an FTP server directly accessible over the Internet is not the best place to house such valuable information.

- Why did it take the company over a year to notice the theft? If use was limited to internal staff only, then why was the company not monitoring the server for access from unfamiliar Internet Protocol (IP) addresses, or using related security techniques?

These questions are particularly relevant, given that FTP security vulnerabilities are well known. For example, the CERT Coordination Center (a non-commercial institution that tracks and advises on information security incidents) issued a public advisory in 1993 in response to "a continuous stream of reports from sites that are experiencing unwanted activities within" their FTP areas. The advisory identified "improper configurations leading to system compromise" as one of the leading causes of the security breaches. The advisory also provided instructions on how to configure FTP to combat certain vulnerabilities.[146]

Auditing or Monitoring May Be Required by Law

Several laws and regulations require Information Management auditing and monitoring programs. Internal Revenue Service Revenue Procedure 97-22 is an excellent example of such a regulation.

Internal and External Audits: IRS Revenue Procedure 97-22

This IRS regulation provides requirements for taxpayers who wish to keep required records in electronic form, and describes several criteria that an electronic recordkeeping system must meet. Moreover, the regulation explicitly requires Information Management-style controls and audits.

For example, the regulation makes clear that an electronic storage system for records must include:

- **Security and other management controls.** "[R]easonable controls to ensure the integrity, accuracy, and reliability of the electronic storage system."

- **Monitoring programs.** "[R]easonable controls to prevent and detect the unauthorized creation of, addition to, alteration of, deletion of, or deterioration of electronically stored books and records."

- **Auditing programs.** "[A]n inspection and quality assurance program evidenced by regular evaluations of the electronic storage system including periodic checks of electronically stored books and records."[147]

The regulation also makes clear that the IRS has the right to periodically conduct its own audit of the taxpayer's recordkeeping system to ensure that it complies. This audit can be quite extensive and may include:

- **System evaluation.** "[A]n evaluation (by actual use) of a taxpayer's equipment and software."

- **Evaluation of procedures.** "[P]rocedures used by a taxpayer to prepare, record, transfer, index, store, preserve, retrieve, and reproduce electronically stored documents."

- **Additional review** of "internal controls, security procedures, and documentation."[148]

In addition, the IRS expects that organizations will also conduct their own Information Management audits. The regulation states that organizations that have converted original hard copy records to electronic form for storage may destroy the hard copy records only after they have completed an internal audit and established an ongoing auditing program.

> This revenue procedure permits the destruction of the original hardcopy books and records and the deletion of the original computerized records... after the taxpayer:
>
> (1) has completed its own testing of the electronic storage system that establishes that hardcopy or computerized books and records are being reproduced in compliance with all the provisions of this revenue procedure, and
>
> (2) has instituted procedures that ensure its continued compliance with all the provisions of this revenue procedure.[149]

Organizations can learn from the model used by the IRS in reviewing electronic record storage systems. It focuses on key areas of internal controls, policies and procedures, and actual system functionality—areas that are critical for any form of Information Management auditing or monitoring program.

Monitoring Programs: "Supervision" Under NASD Conduct Rule 3010

The National Association of Securities Dealers (NASD), in conjunction with the Securities and Exchange Commission and other bodies, regulates the securities industry. The NASD promulgates "Conduct Rules" by which its members must abide. The financial services industry in general and the securities industry specifically, are viewed as among the most regulated industries, and so their approach to regulatory compliance is closely watched by other industries.

One of the NASD's key Conduct Rules for securities brokers and dealers is Conduct Rule 3010, which outlines a primary philosophy of the NASD regulations—that its members have an obligation to actively supervise the activities of their employees on an *ongoing basis*.

The NASD requires that its members "establish and maintain a system to supervise the activities [of employees] that is reasonably designed to achieve compliance with applicable securities laws and regulations." In other words, an auditing and monitoring program. This rule, as it has been interpreted, applies to the supervision of employee email correspondence.

Key elements of the NASD's mandated supervisory system include:

- Written procedures, including records showing to whom supervisory responsibilities were delegated in the organization (see page 163 for a detailed discussion on proper delegation). Companies are also required to keep their procedures up-to-date with "applicable securities laws and regulations."

- An "Internal Inspection," at least annually, which is "reasonably designed to assist in detecting and preventing violations of and achieving compliance with applicable securities laws and regulations." In other words, an internal audit.

- The creation of an office with specific responsibility for over-seeing the supervisory program.

Internal Versus External Auditing and Monitoring Programs

While organizations need to adopt ongoing internal programs for auditing and monitoring their IMC, they also need to consider the role that independent third parties play in auditing and monitoring.

In some cases, organizations should consider the use of independent third parties to conduct period reviews and assessments of their Information Management program. This is particularly the case in highly regulated industries. For example, independent audits and assessments are common in the pharmaceutical industry (using 21 CFR Part 11, for example), the healthcare industry (using HIPAA), and the securities industry (using SEC 17a-4).

Such audits can be very formal and involve multiple steps, including a complete review of Information Management documentation, employee interviews, examination of "live" processes and technology in action, and so on. On the other hand, such audits can also be less formal, and limited to an offsite review of specific policies and proce-dures, for example.

The type of audit that is appropriate depends on many factors, includ-ing the stage that the target organization is in with their Information Management program; the size and number of locations and business units; the complexity of their technology environment; and the legal and regulatory environment in which they operate. For example, an organization that has just completed a revision of its Records Management manual, updated their retention schedule, and intro-duced a new email archiving system is an organization that could like-ly benefit a great deal from an independent assessment of their Information Management program.

There are many models used for independent auditing and assess-ment, and their sources and methodologies vary by industry, audi-ence, and intended result. For example, the American Bar Association has developed the *PKI Assessment Guidelines*, which provides a model for assessing the trustworthiness of an information security system. This document provides a multidisciplinary assessment model that borrows from auditing and risk assessment models used in a variety of contexts, from the insurance industry to computer hardware testing and certification. Effective audits of Information Management programs at most large organizations similarly require a multidisciplinary approach that incorporates specialized legal, technological, Records Management, and other best-practices expertise.

Blurring the Lines

Increasingly the line between public accounting audits and Information Management-related audits is becoming blurred, due in part to Sarbanes-Oxley and related factors. Sarbanes-Oxley Section 404, for example, requires "each registered public accounting firm that prepares or issues the audit report for [a public company]... shall attest to, and report on, the assessment made by the management of [the public company]."

The "assessment made by the management" here refers to the report that Sarbanes-Oxley requires management to include in their annual report that addresses the company's "internal control structure and procedures for financial reporting."

In other words, the Sarbanes-Oxley requires the auditors to do an assessment of an assessment. At a minimum, then, it seems likely that public accounting firms will seek information from that public company that gives them comfort that the internal controls and procedures used by the company are adequate to ensure the financial information's accuracy—which could take them into various other Information Management areas.

Required Third-Party Involvement

In some cases, an organization may be legally required to seek out the validation of a third-party. For example, SEC Rule 17 CFR §240.17a-4 ("17a-4") requires broker-dealer firms that wish to store electronic records on certain types of media to "provide its own representation or one from the storage medium vendor or other third-party with appropriate expertise that the selected storage media meets the conditions" of the regulation. Whether the firm prepares its own representation or has the vendor prepare it, the firm may be placed in a position of relying on a third-party's validation and auditing procedures.

Also, IRS Revenue Procedure 97-22, explored in detail elsewhere in this chapter, specifically states that taxpayers who use a third-party service for storing their records are not relieved of their responsibility to ensure that the requirements of the Revenue Procedure are met. This means that the service provider should expect customers to request contractual assurances that their systems and procedures comply with IRS requirements, which in turn will require the service provider to conduct an internal audit, at a minimum.

Making Representations to Third Parties

On some occasions your organization may be required to make representations about your Information Management program to regulators, courts, auditors, and other third parties. The accuracy of your representations depends in large part on your ability to audit and monitor compliance with your own Information Management policies and procedures. In addition, the third-party may require specific auditing and monitoring activities to ensure that your organization complies with its requirements.

As noted earlier, Sarbanes-Oxley requires public companies to make representations in their annual reports about their "internal control structure and procedures for financial reporting." These companies have to implement and operate extensive auditing and monitoring procedures to ensure that those representations are accurate and will not be a source of future liability.

Another instance where Information Management auditing and monitoring is essential for making representations to a third-party is the U.S. Department of Commerce Safe Harbor program for privacy protection.

In 1998, the European Union (EU) passed the European Commission's Directive on Data Protection, (the "Directive") which among other things does not allow the transfer of personal information from European Union nations to any nation that does not meet the Directive's "standard of adequacy" for privacy protection. The Directive would have made some operations difficult for U.S. companies operating in EU countries, as it would prohibit them from transferring personal information regarding their European customers, for example, to their facilities in the U.S.

The U.S. Department of Commerce, in consultation with the European Commission, developed the Safe Harbor program to address this situation. Safe Harbor effectively allows U.S. companies to comply with the Directive by adjusting their privacy practices to conform to the principles of the Directive. Companies that want to participate must complete an annual "self-certification" that represents to the Department of Commerce (and the public) that its privacy practices conform to the Safe Harbor framework.

The Safe Harbor contains seven "Privacy Principles" that companies must adhere to.[150] One of these principles, entitled "Enforcement," clarifies the need for auditing and monitoring programs to achieve compliance:

> Effective privacy protection must include mechanisms for assuring compliance with the Principles… and consequences for the organization when the Principles are not followed. At a minimum, such mechanisms must include… follow up procedures for verifying that the attestations and assertions businesses make about their privacy practices are true and that privacy practices have been implemented as presented.[151]

The Department of Commerce (DOC) also provides companies with guidance on the "mechanisms for compliance" that they should use, which include Information Management auditing and monitoring programs. DOC states that companies can use "self-assessment or outside compliance reviews" that include such techniques as "random reviews, use of 'decoys,' or use of technology tools as appropriate."[152]

Piracy: Don't Look the Other Way

According to the Business Software Alliance, two out of every five business applications installed on workplace computers today are pirated, resulting in an annual loss of $13 billion to the software industry.[155] Although many companies have turned a blind eye to—or even implicitly endorsed—the common practice of installing a single licensed copy of a software program on multiple computers, in recent years software companies and lawmakers have become more aggressive about preventing this type of piracy.

It may be time to conduct a licensing audit, especially if Information Management assessments and audits are planned. For example, an inventory of the various types of electronic records created throughout an organization will also reveal much information about the software applications in use. This information can in turn be cross-referenced against vendor licensing agreements.

However, as with many issues, legal liability may be greater for organizations that fail to take steps to stamp out internal piracy once they know it exits. This means that you must be prepared to take action through policy, education, discipline, and other measures to deal with any piracy you may find.

Preventing piracy begins with creating the right culture. Your organization needs to send clear messages that piracy is not OK, and educate managers to promote this attitude.

Action Items

- Make sure you have clear statements from senior management forbidding piracy. These are often appropriate coming from the CIO's office, particularly when issued in advance of a licensing audit, and should be included in employee policies and educational materials.

- Especially in small to medium-sized companies with limited IT budgets and centralized IT controls, watch out for employees installing pirated software on their own.

- Work to prevent your company from becoming a source for external piracy. Software applications purchased under a site license may have "copy protections" removed, which makes them easy to copy and disseminate. Closely monitor the use of such installation disks and store them in a secure location.

- Applications provided by business partners can also be pirated, as copy protections are often disabled or reduced, and employees may feel the business relationship entitles them to use the application for free. However, unless such use is explicitly covered by partnership agreements, do not assume that it is permitted.

Monitoring Employee Activity

Information that can be found and logged on employee computers include:

- A record of every software application that was run

- Both sides of Instant Message and chat conversations

- Text and images that were copied to the clipboard

- Keystroke monitoring—a record of every key pressed on a keyboard, and the window in which they were pressed

- A log of processor and memory load, processes running at any given time, and the temperature of the computer's CPU

- Every website visited and the pages that were viewed or other information that was downloaded

- The names of all documents printed

- Internal network locations visited

- Presence monitoring, i.e., determining whether or not a person is "at" their computer (by detecting if keys are being depressed or the mouse is moving), and how much time in a given time period they were using their computer

For better or worse, virtually every activity on a user's computer can be recorded, either by gathering information from installed mainstream applications and the operating system, or from programs specifically installed to monitor user activities.

Using technology to monitor employee activity is fraught with a range of HR, legal, policy, ethical, and other issues. At a minimum, however, organizations need to be aware of the existence of the information created by employees in the course of using company-provided technology. Because, whether you like it or not, such information is likely to be used by the other side in litigation and investigations to the extent that they can find it and it reveals incriminating activity.

Furthermore, whether an organization chooses to use such technology or not, organizations need to be aware of the existence of monitoring tools. Organizations in the past have discovered such tools being used by competitors to spy on their activities and in the context of other damaging circumstances.

Key #6

Effective and Consistent Program Enforcement

Information Management program policies and procedures must be consistently enforced through appropriate disciplinary mechanisms and the proper configuration and management of Information Management-related systems.

Key Overview

> *The existence of a compliance program is not sufficient, in and of itself, to justify not charging a corporation for criminal conduct undertaken by its officers, directors, employees, or agents. Indeed, the commission of such crimes in the face of a compliance program may suggest that the corporate management is not adequately enforcing its program.*
>
> "Federal Prosecution of Corporations," U.S. Department of Justice[156]

Key 5 addressed the need for organizations to employ Information Management auditing and monitoring programs to measure compliance and detect program violations. This section explores what happens next: Once violations are detected, how should they be dealt with?

Chapter 17:

Addressing Employee Policy Violations

IMC recognizes that employees will violate policies and procedures. In some cases, they will do it willfully, despite being fully aware of the consequences. In other cases, violations result from an organization's failure in some aspect of its Information Management program development and implementation.

The reasons that Information Management program violations occur and vary, include the following:

- **Lack of awareness.** Employees were unaware of the policy or procedure, due to inadequate communication and dissemination.

- **Confusion.** Employees were confused about what the policy meant or which policy applied to them, as a result of changes in organizational structure, changes in job roles and responsibilities, undue complexity, lack of training, or other factors.

- **Inconsistent enforcement and lack of oversight.** Policies were not consistently enforced, so employees believed they did not have to comply with them.

- **Willful acts.** Employees deliberately violated the policy out of self-interest and/or criminal intent.

Make Sure Employees Understand the Consequences

Organizations must be crystal clear with employees about the consequences of violating Information Management policies and procedures. Statements outlining consequences should be a standard part of the policies to which they relate, and should be highlighted, communicated, and re-communicated. In other words, these statements should become a standard part of the corporate culture of which every employee is keenly aware.

Sample "Consequences" Policy Statement

VIOLATION OF ANY ASPECT OF THIS POLICY MAY RESULT IN DISCIPLINARY ACTION, UP TO AND INCLUDING TERMINATION. Further, theft or assisting another in theft of any Company property, including Company Records, is a crime for which you may be criminally prosecuted. As such, you must read and follow this Policy, and seek clarification from your supervisor if you are unclear on any requirement. In addition, be aware that this Policy provides MINIMUM STANDARDS. Your department may provide additional and/or different directives that are required to ensure compliance with specific laws, regulations, and industry requirements.

© 2004, Randolph A. Kahn, ESQ., and Barclay T. Blair. For informational purposes only. Seek the advice of counsel before adopting any Information Management policy element.

There are a variety of tools and techniques that organizations can use to help ensure that employees get the message. These include:

- Use an acknowledgement or certification process that requires employees to "sign off" that they have read and understood the policy, and understand the consequences of violating the policy.

- Inform employees that Information Management policies are subject to revision and updating.

- Provide a mechanism for employees to air grievances and seek clarifications related to the Information Management program.

- Consider how your organization will handle "whistleblowers" who bring violations to management's attention.

Sample Employee "Certification" Statement

Signing this document will certify that I have read and understand the "Records Management Manual." I also understand that our Company is committed to protecting its Records and fully complying with all applicable laws and regulations. I will comply with any requirement to preserve Records pursuant to any Records Hold Order or in conjunction with any audit, investigation, or litigation.

I understand that violation of any aspect of this policy may result in disciplinary action, up to and including termination. I understand that when I have a concern about a possible violation of this Policy, I have a duty to report the concern to my supervisor. I further understand that this Policy may be modified from time to time by the Company.

© 2004, Randolph A. Kahn, ESQ., and Barclay T. Blair. For informational purposes only. Seek the advice of counsel before adopting any Information Management policy element.

Inform Employees of Past Violations

It is important that organizations inform current employees of past violations of Information Management policies that have resulted in employee termination and other disciplinary actions. The reason for such communications is to provide a warning to all employees and to prevent further violations, not to embarrass or humiliate the employees who have been disciplined. As such, these communications, whether in the form of an email memo, verbal presentation, or other media, should be professional and focus on how employees can avoid similar situations.

- Do not use the disciplined employees' names, unless there is a very compelling reason to do so, and only with approval of the HR and Legal departments.

- Clearly describe the violation that took place, and if applicable, why it took place and the consequences to the employee.

- Refer to and/or quote the sections of company policy and/or laws that were violated.

- Describe the real or potential harm caused to the company by such violations.

- Describe what employees can do to avoid committing similar violations.

- Remind employees of the importance of the Information Management program as a whole.

The courts have made clear that not only do organizations have the right to communicate with their employees about such matters, but also it is in their interests to do so.

This idea was recently tested in *Garrity v. John Hancock Mut. Life Ins. Co.*,[157] where terminated employees sued their former employer for defamation after company supervisors told "former co-workers, and... employees in other departments, that plaintiffs were terminated for sending and receiving 'sexually lewd, harassing'... and 'sexually explicit' emails."

The court clarified that, even if the statements made by the supervisors rose to the level of defamation, the employer has the right to "disclose defamatory information about employees and former employees," including "an employer's statements of opinions and facts, and statements that an employer reasonably believes to be true."

The fired employees claimed that "no legitimate business purpose was served by disseminating these statements among such a large group of employees." However, the court disagreed, and stated:

To the contrary, all Hancock employees are subject to its email policy. Therefore, defendant had an obvious legitimate business purpose, as to all employees, if it so chose—to warn them and thereby prevent any recurrence of the events that led to this lawsuit.

Email Policy Enforcement

There are many cases in which organizations had good policies in place, but had no good system to ensure that their policies were followed.

For example, a global chemical company had a policy in place that prohibited use of the company email system for sending, receiving, and viewing pornography and violent images. Following a complaint that workers were violating the email policy by sharing pornography, among other prohibited content, the company was forced to fire about 50 experienced employees.

If the company had a good monitoring mechanism in place, the problem could have been identified before the violations were widespread, and one or two employees could have been disciplined—sending a message to the rest of the company and avoiding the disruption and scandal that ensued.

Enforcement Must Be Consistent

Consistency is central to effective Information Management program enforcement. Here's why:

- **Commitment.** Consistency tells employees that you are committed to the Information Management program, so, by implication, they too should be.

- **Clarity.** Consistency minimizes confusion about what will happen if policies are violated, thereby working to increase compliance.

- **Communication.** Consistency tells the outside world, including courts, regulators, auditors, and shareholders, that you take your Information Management obligations seriously.

- **Comfort.** Consistency helps to give customers and partners comfort in doing business with you.

- **Credibility.** Consistency makes enforcement easier for supervisors, managers, and the lawyers by making clear that the company does what it says it will do to ensure that employees do the right thing.

- **Fairness.** Consistency means all violators are treated equally, without favoritism or discrimination.

Although the benefits of consistent program enforcement are clear, many organizations continue to selectively enforce Information Management policies and procedures. While policies need to be somewhat flexible in order to be practical, variation from those directives must be reasonable and explainable.

For example, if an organization finds that employees are constantly violating its email policy that requires them to keep their email inboxes under a mandated size limit, the organization should investigate the cause, rather than simply turning a blind eye to the policy violation. Perhaps the limit is too restrictive, or the size issue is merely symptomatic of larger issues. Maybe employees are retaining too many email messages, or are ignoring email retention policies altogether. A failure to enforce formal written policy not only sends the wrong message to employees, but in this example, leads to increased storage cost and an increased chance that unnecessary email messages will remain in the email system long after they should have been disposed of in the ordinary course of business.

The Risks of Inconsistency

Establishing a consistent approach to enforcement helps to protect organizations from claims by accused violators that they are being selectively, unfairly, or discriminately singled out and disciplined while other violators are not disciplined for the same violation.

For example, in the employment action related to *Autoliv Asp v. Dep't of Workforce Servs*,[158] a state employment board was asked to consider whether or not two employees were terminated for just cause after they violated their employer's policies by sending sexually explicit and offensive email messages through the company email system.

The company's computer use policy specifically prohibited "use of email for reasons other than transmittal of business related information" and "conduct that reflects unfavorably on the corporation." In addition, the company had general rules of conduct and an anti-harassment policy that specified termination as a possible result of violation.

Before the employees were fired, the company had grown concerned about problems caused by excessive volume on the corporate email system. Following an audit of email use, the company determined that employees were using the system for a number of non-business related activities. Following this discovery, the employer sent three company-wide email notifications (including one from the VP of Human Resources), reminding employees that they were required to use the email system only for business-related purposes, and that a failure to do so could result in termination.

Following a complaint from a former employee about receiving sexually harassing email from current employees, the company investigated, found that two employees had sent a number of sexually explicit and offensive email messages, and fired them for "improper and unauthorized use of company email."

The terminated employees did not deny sending the email messages, but claimed that they were unaware that their conduct would result in termination. Subsequent hearings sided with the employees, in large part because the employer had inconsistently enforced their own email policy.

For example, hearings related to the case found that,

- "Because the written policy against excessive email was not consistently enforced the claimants had no knowledge of the expected conduct."

- "Abuse of the company email was common among employees."

- "The company's strict written policy on email use differed from its actual application of that policy."[159]

The company had effectively shot itself in the foot. On the one hand, they had policies that were well thought out, and they effectively communicated those policies to employees. On the other hand, they had allowed the policies to be flagrantly violated for some time, likely because they had neither the resources nor inclination to take enforcement action, until they encountered a performance problem in the email system. The inconsistent enforcement of their own policies enabled the terminated employees to raise doubt as to whether or not the policies were "real" and needed to be taken seriously, and thus dragged them into a legal battle in what should have otherwise been a straightforward case.

Common Inconsistencies

In our consulting practice we have the opportunity to see first hand how organizations enforce their Information Management policies and practices. Our experience shows that there are many areas where organizations fail to enforce consistently. Some of these areas are explored below.

1) **Special treatment for some.** In too many organizations, Information Management policies and practices simply don't seem to apply to some employees. For example, executives are sometimes allowed to delete email messages that have Information Management significance, or are allowed to keep copies of email in personal electronic and hardcopy archives long past their retention periods. While there may be some business justification for treating some executive email differently from that of other employees on an ongoing basis, such treatment should be formally codified in policy and consistently enforced. In some cases, employees or entire departments are allowed to flout Information Management policies. The marketing department exceeds email mailbox sizes because they are sending around big presentations and graphics. The research department trans-

mits big CAD files, and so on. While there may be a reason to vary the rules, generally the rules should be uniform across the company and then consistently enforced.

2) **"Unspoken" or de facto policies.** Some employees are allowed to purchase and use PDAs, messaging-enabled cell phones, and other devices on their own, despite a lack of policies addressing these technologies. In one company, the VP of sales had given his blessing to the sales team using a free P2P file sharing tool to share confidential sales presentations amongst the team, despite the fact that outsiders could hack into and download the presentations at will. Because of the ramifications caused by unofficial, off-policy practices, it is worthwhile to take the time to negotiate a real policy if one is needed.

3) **Neglected back-office operations.** Some companies seem to believe that what happens in the back-office doesn't affect Information Management. For example, we saw a company make an exception to its policy and allow its employees to overwrite back-up tapes containing email before the end of the retention periods, "just this once," simply because they had run out of back-up tapes for that day's back-up run. (As mentioned before, a company was penalized for this kind of activity in *Applied Telematics v. Sprint.*) In another case, the IT staff failed to overwrite email back-up tapes after the end of their retention periods. In *Murphy Oil USA, Inc. v. Fluor Daniel, Inc.*, the company had a 45-day retention period, but back-up tapes containing 14 months of email were found during discovery.

When Inconsistency Becomes Discriminatory

Consider a scenario where a company has an Internet use policy that says Internet use should be for business purposes only. However, the company has turned a blind eye to frequent violations, as long as Internet access is not abused. A worker who returned from retirement is reprimanded for the time he spends searching the Web. In the policy violation review meeting that ensues, the elderly gentleman points out that "everyone" uses the Internet in violation of company policy, and he feels singled out because it takes him longer to read through online pages. If the company chose to formally discipline or even terminate him due to Internet overuse, he may be able to sue for age discrimination.

The courts have made clear that "discriminatory enforcement of a lawful policy is, of course, unlawful."[160]

Chapter 18:

Using Technology to Enforce Policy

An organization's Information Management policies and procedures can be divided into those that require "manual" auditing, monitoring, and enforcement to ensure compliance, and those that can be automatically monitored and enforced using information technology. For example, an email policy that restricts email attachments to 2 MB can be enforced easily by configuring the email server to reject larger attachments. In much the same way, a policy statement that requires employees to "encrypt all email sent outside the company" clearly relies upon the proper configuration and management of an encryption system. If the system is not available or useable, employees cannot comply with the policy.

This section focuses on the latter category of policies and procedures, and explores techniques that all organizations should be aware of when endeavoring to ensure that such directives are effectively and consistently enforced.

Which Directives Can Be "Automatically" Enforced?

Organizations should anticipate the kinds of Information Management program violations they are likely to face, and how they will address such violations when they occur. An exercise that can be helpful in this regard is identifying those policy elements that can be enforced "automatically" through proper configuration and management of information technology. We use the term "automatically" with caution here, because all technology, no matter how advanced or sophisticated, still relies on humans for its proper configuration and management, even if it is a simple as just "flipping a switch."

New and powerful enterprise auditing and monitoring tools are continuously being developed. Those who have received calls from their credit card company after making an unusually large purchase using the card, or from their phone company after making an expensive long distance call across the world for the first time, can attest to this. These companies employ sophisticated monitoring technology that alerts personnel when unusual transactions occur within your account, effectively helping them enforce anti-fraud policies.

It is simply not feasible, though, to automatically track and enforce each employee's compliance with Information Management policies and procedures. After all, it is technically possible to create log files and other "electronic trails," which show how employees have been using company systems. It is another matter having the tools, people, and time to make sense of all that information.

Password policies are a great example—some aspects of which can be automatically enforced, and some of which cannot. For example, a good password policy should dictate the characteristics of allowable passwords, such as the following:

- Passwords must contain uppercase, lowercase, and numeric characters

- Passwords must be at least six characters long

- Passwords must not contain your username

The software applications used to validate and accept network, email, and other usernames and passwords can automatically enforce each of these policy elements. As such, there is little need to manually audit or monitor user password formation, aside from ensuring that the software used to validate passwords is properly configured and operational.

However, there are common password policy elements that cannot be automatically enforced, so there is a need to monitor and audit compliance with those elements. For example, good password policies should address issues such as the following:

- Under no circumstances are employees allowed to share their password with anyone inside or outside the company, even if such sharing is to provide temporary access to a colleague or "cover" for someone out of the office.

- Passwords should never be written down, emailed, spoken, or communicated in any way to anyone inside or outside the company, including administrative assistants and managers.

- Passwords should not be based on personal information, such as date of birth, a child or spouse's name, social security number, or any other information that could be easily guessed ("socially engineered") by someone who knows you or who has access to personal information about you.

- Passwords should never be displayed, stored, or concealed in your workspace.

Those policy elements cannot be automatically enforced by company systems. However, they are of equal, if not greater, importance to the company's overall information security program. As such, a company needs to develop a method to audit and monitor employee compliance with these directives that includes elements such as:

- Periodic manual review of a statistical sampling of employee passwords conducted by qualified and designated IT personnel

- Periodic inspection of a statistical sampling of employee's physical workspace to see if passwords are on display

- Periodic employee surveys regarding the use of passwords, to gauge compliance

The section below provides a number of sample policy elements and a discussion of how such elements may be automatically enforceable.

Sample Policy Element #1: Email Content

All email must be written in a professional manner, and should be free of profanity and sexually explicit content.

Automatically Enforceable?

To some extent.

How?

Although most people have at least an instinctive sense of what "written in a professional manner" means, it is sufficiently subjective that teaching it to a computer would be difficult. However, email content filtering technology is readily available that can look for profanity, sexual language, and other triggers that might indicate that a message contains prohibited content.

This technology is used in many freely downloadable "spambusting" types of programs that are designed to identify and block spam. Aside from looking for specific words, these programs often use sophisticated Bayesian logic that looks at a wide variety of factors in making a determination about whether or not an email is spam, including its size, content, sender, subject line formation, and other factors. The same basic technology can also be deployed on an enterprise-wide basis to block or quarantine suspect messages, thereby providing effective automatic enforcement of one element of a company's email policy.

Sample Policy Element #2: Software Use

Employees are not allowed to download, install, or operate any software on company-supplied computers and devices that has not been supplied by the IT department. Unauthorized software can create security risks and legal liability issues for the company.

Automatically Enforceable?

Yes.

How?

Companies can use a variety of technologies and techniques to prevent all but the most sophisticated users from installing and using unauthorized software. For example, many operating systems can be configured to only allow IT administrators to install software. Operating systems can also be configured to only allow installation of software programs found on the company's network, and not on the user's local hard drive. In addition, specialty programs can perform automatic auditing of a computer connected to the company network, and monitor and catalogue software used over the Internet or internal network. Although no method is foolproof, these technologies or techniques can help an organization enforce these kinds of policy elements.

Sample Policy Element #3:
File Sharing and Instant Messaging

Employees are not allowed, under any circumstances, to use peer-to-peer (P2P) file sharing programs to download or upload files of any type from the Internet or within the corporate network. Use of such technology may create security risks and subject the company to legal liability.

Automatically Enforceable?

Yes.

How?

Organizations can monitor the traffic flowing over their own networks and onto the Internet using a variety of tools and techniques, including firewalls and network/bandwidth monitoring software. These tools can be used to recognize and/or block certain types of network traffic, such as P2P file sharing applications. Organizations with policy elements preventing the use of specific communications technologies such as P2P file sharing and Instant Messaging, for example, can use these tools to automatically enforce compliance with such directives by controlling and/or blocking their use.

Similar techniques could also be used to block Instant Messaging traffic from leaving the company's internal network in order to enforce a policy element such as the following:

Although the company provides Instant Messaging facilities for you to use, Instant Messaging is only to be used for communicating with other employees, and is never to be used to communicate with clients, partners, or any outside parties under any circumstance.

Sample Policy Element #4: Records Hold

No documents, communications, or Records subject to Records Hold may be altered, disposed of, erased, or otherwise made inaccessible, whether in paper or electronic form, for any reason whatsoever. Failure to preserve Business Information specified in a Legal Hold can subject the Company, its Associates, and third parties to fines, sanctions, criminal conviction, including being incarcerated, and other legal penalties.

Automatically Enforceable

No.

Why?

A Records Hold is a complex process that may involve dozens, if not hundreds of employees and thousands of pieces of information that may have to be preserved. It should not be thought of as a policy element or process that is "automatically" enforceable using information technology. That being said, technology can play a big role in the Records Hold process, such as:

- using the corporate intranet to disseminate Records Hold information to ensure that employees understand their preservation obligations;

- preventing unauthorized destruction or alteration of responsive records;

- collecting and preserving responsive records and other electronic information in electronic form;

- copying responsive material from employee hard drives and network file locations; and/or,

- finding and producing material from company databases, document management systems, Records Management software systems, and so on.

Managing the Administrators

Let's face it: The more that an organization depends on information technology in its Information Management program, the more the organization relies on the talents, training, experience, and ethics of its IT staff and administrators. There is an entire realm of Information Management-related policies and procedures that specifically apply to the work that IT administrators do that also must be consistently enforced. And the people doing the enforcing have to be knowledgeable enough about the technology to make an accurate assessment of compliance.

After all, it is the "trusted insider" who is usually capable of causing the most harm at an organization, whether due to negligence, incompetence, or malicious intent. To put it another way, how does a company protect itself from someone who not only has all the keys to the building, but also designed the locks? The more technology-savvy an employee, the more likely it is that they will be able to flout Information Management policies and procedures and get away with it.

Tech Bosses Need to Be Tech-Savvy

A flaw in the design and controls of an off-track betting system in New York for horse racing was recently exploited to the tune of $3 million. A delay between the time bets were made by bettors and when bets were received and finalized by the central betting system allowed an insider to change bets to name the winning horses of races that had already been run. Had the company's supervisors been as capable with the technology as the employee who recognized the flaw and exploited it, there is a good chance that the fraud could have been avoided.

As it pertains to information security specifically, there are a number of techniques used by organizations to minimize the amount of damage that a trusted insider would be capable of doing, such as requiring the collaboration of two or more parties for sensitive security operations. A well-designed program for hiring employees who will be given access to such sensitive information and processes should also be employed.

Organizations might have well-researched and well-written internal policies that dictate how IT administrators should configure and manage information technology, but these policies will do little good unless companies are able to ensure that IT staff is consistently applying these policies in the real world. Information technology touches nearly every aspect of Information Management in most companies today, which means that IMC largely relies on IT professionals to properly configure and manage IT systems.

Key #7

Continuous Program Improvement

When improper management of information is detected, the organization must take all reasonable steps to respond appropriately to the activity and to prevent further similar activities—including any necessary modifications to its Information Management Program.

Key Overview

Continuous program improvement is the last of the Seven Keys to IMC. You must continuously improve and update your Information Management program and adapt it to changes in your business, new laws and regulations, and problems and weaknesses that are discovered through your auditing and monitoring programs.

Chapter 19:

The Ongoing Work of IMC

If there is one overarching message that readers should take away from this book, it is that IMC is a process, not a project. While the "process" of IMC can certainly be broken down into "projects" where much of the work is done in their initial phases (i.e., drafting policies and procedures), even those activities require ongoing review, updating, and improvement.

Every organization must strive to continually improve its Information Management program. Every program has flaws and weaknesses that need to be addressed. Every program goes out of date with current best practices, laws, and technology unless it is continuously revised and revisited. Every program can be better.

Why Is Continuous Program Improvement (CPI) Required?

Organizations must continue to update and change their Information Management program in order to ensure that it keeps doing its job. That job is to protect and promote the organization's legal and business interests.

A recent study conducted by AIIM International and Kahn Consulting, Inc.,[161] revealed a number of reasons why organizations update their Information Management practices. Organizations that were planning to make changes (or had made changes) to the way that they managed email listed the following as reasons for the change:

- The increasing volume of email in their organizations (46%)

- Lawsuits, business losses, viruses, system downtime, or other damages their organization had directly experienced (30%)

- The Sarbanes-Oxley Act (20%)

- High-profile media coverage of business failures and corporate malfeasance (20%)

- The increasing use of email messages in litigation, audits, and investigations (30%)

These survey results provide insight into the various reasons that organizations update and change their Information Management practices. While the specific drivers of change are always evolving, the reasons that organizations need to continuously improve their programs are relatively constant, and include:

- **Addressing flaws and failures.** Addressing flaws that were discovered through auditing and monitoring; that were brought to the attention of the organization through a grievance process; and failures that blossomed into full-fledged legal or regulatory action.

- **Changing business focus.** Adapting to new business strategies, such as a shift from U.S. to European markets, might require a change in the approach to employee and customer privacy protection.

- **Changing technology.** Updating the program to anticipate Information Management issues raised by the use of new kinds of technology, such as Instant Messaging and P2P file sharing.

- **Changing laws and regulations.** Ensuring that program elements comply with new or updated laws and regulations. There have been many new laws and regulations affecting Information Management in recent years, and the pace of lawmaking does not appear to be slowing.

- **Changing best practices.** Best practices are constantly changing in every industry to account for changing market conditions and other factors, and this must be reflected in Information Management policies and practices. For example, while few organizations explicitly addressed email issues in a separate policy, it has become a "best practice" to do so in organizations that rely heavily on email for business purposes.

Changing Technology Means Changing the Program

We conclude that in today's workplace, the email transmission of sexually explicit and offensive jokes, pictures, and videos constitutes a flagrant violation of a universal standard of behavior.

Autoliv Asp v. Dep't of Workforce Servs.[162]

At one time, email use was largely limited to the world of research institutions and defense contractors. Then, with the growing popularity of the World Wide Web, students and other tech-savvy people around the world adopted it. Businesses began to catch on and see the potential of the technology. Over time, of course, the technology has become widespread, with nearly all organizations using it in some form, and many completely reliant on it. Fully 100% of respondents to the AIIM International/Kahn Consulting, Inc. study stated in 2003 that their organizations used email for business purposes.

And they are using it for increasingly sensitive and important tasks. In fact, 71% of organizations surveyed now use email to negotiate contracts and agreements, and 69% use it to exchange invoices, statements, and payment information. Nearly all organizations (93%) use email as a tool for communicating with customers. Moreover, it is not just companies that feel this comfort—regulators and government agencies seem to increasingly be on board too. The survey showed that 38% of organizations use email to respond to regulators, and 44% use it to file with official bodies.

Unfortunately, even as businesses invested heavily in email technology, most did not show the same enthusiasm for updating and adapting

Information Management program policies and procedures to account for the technology. As a result, an avalanche of court cases and legal actions related to the use and misuse of email began, and organizations were forced to retroactively change their Information Management practices. Many learned their lesson the hard way, feeling the pain of harassment lawsuits and mass employee terminations.

Even today, as hard as it may be to believe, there are still a significant number of organizations that fail to address email use in their Information Management policies and procedures. Nearly a quarter of organizations surveyed in the AIIM/KCI survey do not provide employees with formal written policies regarding email, for example.

A Prescription for Pain

In our consulting practice we came across a pharmaceutical company that had implemented an employee PDA program in which every employee in the company received a handheld device with software that had been specifically customized for the firm. It was cutting-edge, visionary, and everyone was excited.

Except the compliance department. Actually, the compliance department didn't feel any emotions about the PDA program because they were not consulted at all.

Several months later, the cutting-edge program was deemed a success. The employees were hooked, and had incorporated the handy little devices into almost every aspect of their working lives.

Then the FDA came knocking. And asked troubling compliance questions.

"Can you explain to us how these PDAs comply with FDA record keeping requirements? How and where exactly is the information on these PDA retained? How is it protected?"

The program was scrapped. Millions of dollars were wasted.

> The company failed horribly in the way they implemented the program, but at least they did one thing right. They realized that the most effective way to "continuously improve" the program was to get rid of it.

Which Technology Is Next?

Have organizations around the world learned their lesson, or are they doomed to repeat the mistakes of the past by implementing new technology without adequate consideration of its Information Management obligations? Only time will tell.

Even a cursory glance at today's technology landscape quickly reveals that there are many technologies that appear to be taking a similar path.

Business use of Instant Messaging has become widespread enough to attract the attention of regulators like the National Association of Securities Dealers, which has told brokers that they need to supervise and retain Instant Messages like any other form of business correspondence. And business users are expected to make up nearly half of the 500 million people that will be using Instant Messaging by 2006.[163]

Instant Messaging has a variety of Information Management implications. Can messages be retained? Is it secure? Should we allow employees to use it to talk to customers, or should it only be for internal purposes? Can we be sued if someone "tells" a dirty joke via an Instant Message? Many of these issues are the same as email, and organizations can certainly build on the work they have done in that area. On the other hand, Instant Messaging presents its own new set of challenges that organizations need to investigate and address, such as the inability to pre-review communications. The question is: Will they? Or will Instant Messaging provide the next wave of Information Management-related lawsuits?

P2P file sharing is another likely candidate. Aside from the security issues created by employees opening a hole in the corporate defenses to share MP3's of their favorite bands using consumer-oriented P2P tools, there are numerous other serious issues, including copyright infringement. One company has already publicly settled a copyright infringement action with the Recording Industry Association of America over the operation of an MP3 file trading network inside the company. While P2P technology is also employed for a wide variety of legitimate business purposes, it creates Information Management issues that must be addressed proactively.

Changes in the technology used in your organization, regardless of how insignificant or informal they may seem today, demand changes in Information Management policies and procedures.

Even the Experts Don't Always Get It Right

In 2003, the U.S. General Accounting Office (GAO) completed a review of the way the National Archives and Records Administration (NARA), our nation's keeper of records, was going about acquiring a system to manage and store electronic records.

NARA had created a plan for acquiring an advanced electronic records archive (ERA) based on the "recognized industry standards set by the Institute of Electrical and Electronics Engineers,"[164] one of the primary standards bodies in the digital world.

However, the GAO found that "key policy and planning documents are missing elements that are required by the standards," resulting in "serious long-term risks to the costs, schedule, and performance."

As a result, NARA's "Chief Information Officer" was required to "take a range of actions" designed to address the shortfalls, including "revising key planning documents."

Dealing with Flaws and Failure

Organizations must have a mechanism in place to deal with Information Management program failures. Failures will happen, and they provide an opportunity for organizations to learn and improve their programs and avoid the mistakes of the past.

Find the True Source of the Failure

Sometimes events that appear to be the cause of a program failure are actually a symptom of a larger problem, so it is important that organizations ensure that they have found the true source of the problem when designing program improvements.

For example, a client recently told us that they had been considering a major investment in network equipment and additional bandwidth to resolve an ongoing problem with a slow corporate network and Internet access that routinely "bogged down." However, before they made the purchase, a member of their IT staff installed and ran a network monitoring program. The program revealed that dozens of employees were using P2P file sharing software, with many employees constantly downloading files over the Internet from the time they got into work until the time they left. The client informed employees that file sharing was not allowed at work, and network performance shortly improved to the point that the additional investment was not required.

Do not assume that violations of Information Management policies are isolated incidents. If one employee is not properly retaining electronic records or is routinely failing to encrypt confidential email messages, for example, it is possible that others are committing the same violation, and such patterns should be investigated through Information Management auditing and monitoring programs.

Take Disciplinary Action

Organizations need to be swift, decisive, and consistent when addressing violations of Information Management policies and practices. Tell employees what will happen if they violate policies and procedures. If employees commit a violation, use the event to learn where your Information Management program may be lacking, and ask hard questions about it. Was the employee properly trained? Could the policy be any clearer? Do we need to communicate more regularly with employees about their Information Management obligations? Use the insights you gain from such incidents to improve your program and minimize the likelihood of such failures occurring again.

Correct the Problem

Correcting Information Management problems is often much more difficult than disciplining a few employees and updating a few policies. In fact, Information Management problems are often systemic and can only be addressed through a complete re-examination of the organization's overall approach. Failures that are related to "big picture" issues, such as a poorly functioning organizational structure or a lack of executive support, extend beyond Information Management specifically and need to be addressed in a different context.

Not every problem is so complex, however. Some problems can be addressed through relatively minor changes to policies or procedures, or by investing in new technology or re-configuring existing technology. For example, network and bandwidth monitoring technology can be a great ally in your effort to enforce policies governing how employees use the Internet, and can be an affordable addition to your arsenal of program enforcement and improvement tools.

Change and Improvement Is Always Needed

With the rush to go electronic, some state and local governments put public records on the Web without first creating policies addressing which records need to be there. After 9/11, that decision has to be revisited in recognition that having certain records online (including architectural plans for buildings) enhances the risk of a terrorist attack. As a result, policy is developed and public records are evaluated on a case-by-case basis to determine what belongs online.

Provide a Mechanism for Inquiries

Any program that requires employee compliance must provide a mechanism for employees to ask questions, seek clarification, and address problems. The Information Management program is no different. Some of the most insightful and useful information about the functioning of the program is likely to come from the people who are applying it every day in a variety of situations that may or may not have been contemplated by the program architects. Remind employees often how they can communicate with the organization about the program, and regularly encourage them to do so (or even reward them for doing so).

Change Management: The Key to Success in Implementing Program Improvements

Change Management is an important aspect of Continuous Program Improvement because at its core, Change Management seeks to address the people aspect of any project or program enhancement. The goal of the organization's Change Management is to ensure the success of program changes by assessing and addressing the impact of those changes on affected groups and individuals. An Information Management program that fails to address Change Management greatly increases its risk of failure.

Characteristics of unsuccessful projects often include one or more of the following:

- Lack of project alignment with overall business strategy

- Poor business requirements identification

- Insufficient buy-in and support from senior management

- Incomplete understanding of how the changes will affect key stakeholder groups (i.e., "what's in it for me")

- Poor communication about the change within the organization, including impacts and benefits

- Failure to budget sufficient resources to address process, communications, and training requirements

To ensure your Information Management program succeeds, it is critical that you closely analyze and address its impact on your employees who play a critical role in making the program successful.

Strategies for Success

There are a number of Change Management strategies that the organization can implement to increase the success of its Information Management program changes and updates.

Here is a list to get you started:

Know your stakeholders. An Information Management program affects individuals and groups in different ways. It is imperative that you take the time to identify the key stakeholders affected by the change, how they will be impacted, and what the benefits of the change are to them. Don't forget to spend the time to analyze stakeholders that are against your program. You will need to think about how to either change the mindset of these stakeholders to support your program, or determine how best to neutralize their ability to slow down/stop your program.

Conduct a high-level gap analysis. Think about the vision of your Information Management program. What does excellence look like? How would the company act under the new program? What processes would be in place? What new roles would need to be established? How would individuals and groups need to change their work habits? What efficiencies/costs savings/cost avoidance would result? Areas to consider include the following:

- New roles and responsibilities
- New procedures and processes
- New tools and systems
- New training and job aids
- New governance models
- New measurements and rewards

Once you've thought about the future (the "To-Be"), identify the gaps (the "As-Is"). Look at some of the key stakeholder groups and, using the focus areas, identify where they are today. By comparing today's world and the future vision you will be able to begin planning the journey.

Develop a compliance management "change roadmap." There's a reason people use maps when they travel in unfamiliar territory. The map helps them identify a route from point "A" to point "B," track their progress along the journey, and adjust as issues and problems arise (road construction, detours, and so on). If you have done a gap analysis the "As-Is" is your starting point; the "To-Be" is your destination.

For each significant stakeholder group you will need a high-level roadmap. Identify tangible tasks/activities that will need to happen to make the change successful for that particular audience.

Once you've completed your group analysis, consolidate your findings into an overall roadmap that summarizes the broad impacts on the organization.

Construct a solid business case. You cannot establish a sense of urgency and interest in your compliance program without the facts. First, make sure your business case aligns with your corporate strategy. This will help greatly when you are getting executive buy-in to the business case. Second, the business case needs to address both quantitative and qualitative reasons for implementing a compliance management program—focus wherever possible on things that tangibly impact the company's bottom-line financials. Cost avoidance (reduced risk of litigation), quicker access to information, efficient reuse of corporate knowledge, and compliance with governmental regulations are all examples of this. Third, do not forget to develop a risk analysis as part of the business case so that people clearly understand the risks involved in the program and how you plan to mitigate these risks. Finally, make sure your business case has a post-implementation measurements process to ensure the benefits you have established in your business case are achieved.

Establish buy-in and leverage "change champions."
Change champions play a critical role both in the compliance
management planning/approval process as well as the implementation. During the approval process you should identify, for
each of the key stakeholder groups, respected individuals with
whom you can review your overall business case and change
impacts and get feedback. Try to find individuals who can be
used as "references" in support of the program. After gathering
this feedback, adjust the roadmap/stakeholder analysis and business case to reflect this feedback.

Once implementation begins, it's critical to directly involve
representatives from the key stakeholder groups in the change
program. Try to draw upon those individuals that you spoke
with when gaining support for your business case. Prior to
identifying these champions, make sure you can set expectations around their roles/responsibilities. These individuals will
need to:

- Provide guidance, insight, and perspective to your implementation, including review of selected deliverables and
  feedback on stakeholder group buy-in, communications
  strategies, and implementation

- Help in the communications process—leveraging the champions to communicate to their respective groups will lend
  additional credibility to your change program

- Participate on any project working committees

Make sure you also try to estimate a time commitment for the
champion, for example 2 to 4 hours per week. This will help to
establish expectations and ensure that the right champions participate in the work effort.

Create a comprehensive communications plan.
Communicate and communicate again. That being said, communicating smartly and targeting your messages requires

thoughtful planning and analysis. See if you can leverage a communications professional within your company as a guide. They can look at your stakeholder analysis and identify key messages, different communications pathways, and the timing of your messages. Don't forget to have as part of the plan a feedback mechanism—have in place different means for getting feedback from your stakeholders and to measure the success of your change efforts.

Identify one or two quick wins to generate positive support and feedback. Is there something in your existing compliance management process that you can change in order to declare an early victory as well as demonstrate your program can generate the agreed-upon benefits? Look for "low hanging fruit," i.e., wins that will generate quick value within a short amount of time and with a small amount of money/resources expended. Early celebration of success and recognition of those individuals/groups involved will build momentum and help increase overall program buy-in.

Evaluate the success or failure of the change with the program sponsor and appropriate change champions. Once you have implemented the program, aggressively focus on benefits realization. Monitor the success metrics established in the business case and make sure that you are achieving the benefits promised. If not, work closely with the program sponsor and appropriate change champions to analyze the issues and make corrections. Change journeys hit a wall that you will need to break through—use your plans and persistence to overcome these post-implementation obstacles and to make your compliance management program a long-term success.

Courtesy of James Hospodarsky, Director of Global Knowledge Management, Dimension Data Holdings plc

Communicating Flaws and Failures

Communicating about Information Management program failures can be tricky business. On the one hand, communicating about weaknesses and failures helps bring the problem to the forefront and sends a message that the organization is committed to solving their problems. On the other hand, admissions of failure can open up an organization to legal liability. Organizations must determine the correct approach on a case-by-case basis. In addition, as explored below, there may be occasions where disclosure may be required by law.

The concept of "corporate accountability and transparency" has become popular in the wake of the many high-profile corporate scandals of the opening years of the new century. The expectation of shareholders and citizens, and indeed of the drafters of laws like Sarbanes-Oxley, is that organizations will be more forthcoming about the problems they face and the risks they represent. They expect greater disclosure of internal problems, and they expect that incompetence will be immediately corrected and fraud will be swiftly and harshly punished.

Only time will tell whether or not the current "culture of accountability and transparency" is transitory or permanent. Regardless of its ultimate effect, organizations will always have to deal with the issue of communicating and disclosing problems that need correcting and even failure.

Self-Critical Analysis Privilege

In select cases, if the results of internal audits and other investigative processes reveal problems in the way an organization conducts its affairs, the organization may be covered by a special form of protection called self-critical analysis privilege. This concept is quite intricate (and still developing and only selectively applied), but on the most basic level, it prevents certain "self audit" information from being used as evidence against the company even if the information is "critical" of its own past actions.

Although the concept of self-critical analysis privilege has been applied (with some restrictions) primarily to protect medical peer reviews concerning the quality of patient care, some have sought to extend its protection to other types of information generated by, or at the request of, an organization, where that information is critical of that organization. For example, courts have extended this protection to "a company's internal assessment of its equal employment opportunity practices" and "for internal reports that evaluate a company's historical compliance with environment regulations."[165]

The basic argument in favor of the self-critical analysis privilege is that it would allow organizations to be unflinchingly candid and thorough in investigating and documenting their internal practices. They would not have to be afraid of what they find out in the course of their internal audits, because the results could not be used against them in court. As a result, the argument goes, the organization's practices will get continuously better over time.

The basic argument against this type of protection is that "the public has a right to every man's evidence."[166] In other words, in order to be fair and just, the judicial system needs to have access to all relevant information in considering each case.

These competing arguments were tested in *Carr v. El Dorado Chem. Co.*[167] where the plaintiff fought to compel production of an internal audit that it believed showed that the defendant was violating environmental laws. The defendant claimed the self-critical analysis privilege with respect to the internal audit, but the court disagreed and allowed the document to be used in the trial, because it believed that the information was necessary for the fair adjudication of the trial.

Competitive Information

The self-critical analysis privilege is only one of the many principles that are used to prevent the disclosure of certain internal company records. For example, companies often argue that revealing certain internal information should be protected because it would benefit competitors if publicly released during legal proceedings.

This principle was tested in Oregon in 2003, where the jury in an antitrust lawsuit found a large lumber firm guilty of anti-competitive behavior, and awarded nearly $80 million in damages to a small sawmill company. The company argued that certain records used in the trial should not be publicly released, as they would help competitors, but the court ruled that the public interest overcame the company's concerns.

The documents included memos that discussed various aspects of the company's success in the market, and even included a PowerPoint presentation allegedly predicting time frames for the demise of competitive sawmills—damaging information in the context of anti-trust litigation.

Communication May Be Required by Law

In the near future, it is unlikely that the self-critical analysis privilege will be widely accepted by courts, or widely used to prevent disclosure of internal "critical analysis." In any event, there are occasions where organizations will be compelled by law to disclose failures to the public.

For example, Sarbanes-Oxley requires a public company's CEO and CFO to certify in each annual and quarterly report that they have reviewed the report, and that the information in the report is true, does not omit important information, and is not misleading. This is a law that appears to require public companies to communicate certain failures.

Another example is SB 1386, a new law that went into effect in the state of California in July 2003, but is expected to have a national impact.

The California law requires organizations to notify the public about security breaches. More specifically, it requires any organization "that owns or licenses computerized data that includes personal information... disclose any breach of the security of the data." The law was developed largely in response to an incident in which hackers accessed California state government computers that contained information on over 200,000 state employees, after which the government took weeks to notify the employees about the incident.

Failure under the law may give rise to lawsuits and monetary damages. Put another way, now companies that do business with California residents, or have their information, not only have to properly manage their personal information but may also have to protect against malicious hackers criminally gaining access to personal information through inadequately secured company computers.

Aside from liability issues, organizations are typically reluctant to provide information on hacking incidents as it may reveal valuable information to competitors about the organization's approach to data management and about its investments in information technology. The effect of SB 1386 on these types of disclosures will be instructive and organizations should watch the development of practices around this law closely.

Conclusion

We are in a business environment where information plays an increasingly important role in the success of both public and private organizations. In our imperfect world, where information is contemporaneously growing in volume and importance, we have ample evidence to take Information Management seriously. In recent times, we have seen IMC failures take a huge toll on countless companies that mismanaged or entirely failed to manage its information assets.

Companies have withered away. State and federal governmental institutions have obliterated already limited budgets trying to comply with recordkeeping laws. Corporations have been suffering through an ample amount of bad press for information mismanagement. And company employees have been accused, convicted, and incarcerated for IMC failures.

We have witnessed a confluence of events that makes a compelling case that what organizations have been doing up to this point may not be good enough.

Policies drafted but not enforced can mean failure. The existence of an Information Management program, but inconsistent application of its directives, can mean failure. Developing the directives, but improperly delegating responsibility for their implementation and enforcement can mean failure. Failing to tell employees to refrain from destroying "anything potentially relevant" or suspend the records retention schedule in the context of an impending lawsuit can also mean failure. Responsibility to prevent these failures begins at the top of organizations and trickles down to all employees.

Successful Information Management today requires a discipline that to this point has been used almost exclusively by the compliance community. IMC is a methodology that applies a compliance framework to all Information Management and is designed to increase the chances that your organization will get it right or provide some insulation when it does not. A half-hearted or unsupported Information Management effort is not good enough. Information Management needs to be done right. We believe IMC and our Seven Keys provides a methodology to help you and your organization get it right.

Mistakes will happen—they always do. IMC is about building an Information Management environment where less can go wrong. It is also about building an environment that minimizes the costs and harm when things do go wrong. Our hope is that Information Management Compliance will also provide you and your organizations with the benefit of the doubt by courts, regulators, bosses, stockholders, and the public when failure strikes. Our hope is that our Seven Keys will help you, and your organization, be more successful.

Notes

Introduction

1. Exhibit B, as provided in a letter from the U.S. House Committee on Energy and Commerce's Subcommittee on Oversight and Investigations to the U.S. Attorney General, December 17, 2002.

2. Eichenwald, Kurt, "Arthur Andersen Convicted of Obstruction of Justice," *The New York Times*, June 15, 2002.

3. United States Sentencing Commission, *Guidelines Manual*, §3E1.1, Nov. 2002.

Chapter 1

4. Lyman, Peter, and Hal R. Varian, "How Much Information," 2003.

5. Jakubowski, Joe, "Protecting the Heart of the Desktop," Storage Network World Online, May 27, 2003.

6. "Worldwide Email Usage Forecast, 2002-2006: Know What's Coming Your Way," IDC Report, as reported by Gretel Johnston, IDG News Service, October 2, 2002.

7. As reported by the World Wireless Forum.

8. "Is IM a Sieve for Corporate Secrets?" IDC as reported by PCWorld.com, July 19, 2002.

9. National Commission on Federal Paperwork in 1977.

10. "Information Management," International Encyclopedia of Information and Library Science, 2nd ed. Edited by John Feather and Paul Sturges. London: Routledge, 2002.

11. Wideman, R. Max, Wideman Comparative Glossary of Common Project Management Terms v3.1, March 2002.

12. U.S. Environmental Protection Agency glossary. Online at http://www.epa.gov/records/gloss/gloss05.htm

13. Aslib, The Association for Information Management glossary. Online at http://www.aslib.com/info/glossary.html

14. AIIM International, "About AIIM." Online at http://www.aiim.org/article_aiim.asp?ID=18274

15. Ibid.

16. ARMA International, "Information Management: A Business Imperative: FAQs for Corporate Executives and Decision Makers," 2002.

17. ARMA International, "Is Strategic Information Management Your Destiny?" October 2000. Online at http://www.arma.org/about/sim_faq.cfm

18. *Murphy Oil USA, Inc. v. Fluor Daniel, Inc.,* 2002 U.S. Dist. LEXIS 3196 (U.S. Dist., 2002).

Chapter 2

19. ISO 15489-11—Information and documentation—Records Management—Part 1: General / ISO, Geneva, 2001.

20. *Moore v. General Motors Corp.,* 558 S.W.2d 720, 736 (Mo. App., 1977).

21. It should be noted that this is only an example, and there may in fact be cases where an organization is obligated to keep all drafts and revisions of a document in order to comply with law or regulation.

22. Federal Rules of Evidence 803(6).

Chapter 3

23. ISO 15489, Information and documentation—Records management, October 2001.

24. NARA, Context for Electronic Records Management. Online at http://www.archives.gov/records_management/policy_and_guidance/baseline_organizational_information_survey.html

25. DoD 5015.2-STD, June 19, 2002.

26. U.S. Environmental Protection Agency glossary. Online at http://www.epa.gov/records/gloss/gloss05.htm

27. Public Law 106-229, Section 101(a)(1).

28. *United States v. Catabran,* 836 F.2d 453, 457 (9th Cir. 1988).

29. *Monotype Corp. PLC v. International Typeface Corp.,* 43 F.3d 443.

30. *Pettiford v. N.C. HHS,* 2002 U.S. Dist. LEXIS 18879.

31. *Sea-Land Serv. v. Lozen Int'l, LLC,* 285 F.3d 808.

32. *Gamber-Johnson, LLC v. Trans Data Net Corp.,* 2001 WI App 224.

33. 17a-4(f)(2)(ii)(A).

34. Section III(B) of SEC Release No. 34-44238, "Commission Guidance to Broker-Dealers on the Use of Electronic Storage Media under the Electronic Signatures in Global and National Commerce Act of 2000 with Respect to Rule 17a-4."

35. SEC Release No. 34-47806, "Electronic Storage of Broker-Dealer Records," May 7, 2003.

Chapter 4

36. International Compliance Association, "Compliance and the Regulatory Environment." Online at http://www.int-comp.org/doc.asp?docId=6920&CAT_ID=676

37. "Federal Prosecution of Business Organizations," Department of Justice Memorandum to Heads of Department Components and United States Attorneys, January 2003.

38. Ibid.

39. Ibid.

40. Fowler, Tom, and Mary Flood, "Arthur Andersen gets the maximum sentence," *Houston Chronicle*, October 16, 2002.

41. "Destruction Of Enron-Related Documents by Andersen Personnel," Hearing Before the Subcommittee On Oversight And Investigations Of The Committee On Energy And Commerce, House Of Representatives, One Hundred Seventh Congress, Second Session, January 24, 2002, Serial No. 107-80.

42. Exhibit B, as provided in a letter from the U.S. House Committee on Energy and Commerce's Subcommittee on Oversight and Investigations to the U.S. Attorney General, December 17, 2002.

43. "Destruction Of Enron-Related Documents by Andersen Personnel," Hearing Before the Subcommittee On Oversight And Investigations Of The Committee On Energy And Commerce, House Of Representatives, One Hundred Seventh Congress, Second Session, January 24, 2002, Serial No. 107-80, p. 166.

44. "Andersen admits to faulty shredding policy," Bloomberg, March 21, 2002.

45. "United States of America against Arthur Andersen, LLP.," Indictment CRH 02-121, Southern District of Texas, March 7, 2002.

46. Hitt, Liewsman, Will, "Andersen Fires Partner It Says Led Shredding of Documents, Brown," *Wall Street Journal*, January 16, 2002.

47. Beltran, Rogers, Gering, "Duncan admits to obstructing justice," CNN/Money, May 14, 2002.

48. Farrell, Greg, "Andersen staffer says phrase was a hint to shred," *USA Today*, May 21, 2002.

49. Thomas, Jr., Landon, as quoted in "U.S. Accuses Top Banker of Obstruction," *New York Times*, April 24, 2003.

50. *Mathias v. Jacobs*, 197 F.R.D. 29, S.D.N.Y., 2000.

51. Ibid.

52. For example, it was reported that Temple sent an email on November 11 directing all U.S. Enron engagement personnel to "ensure that all documents and materials already in existence are preserved," and "any new documents or materials that are created as part of Andersen's continuing work with Enron… are also preserved." Nancy Temple email, subject line, "Enron—Procedures for Responding to Subpoenas and Litigation" to David Duncan and others, November 11, 2001, posted on Findlaw.com.

Chapter 5

53. SEC Press Release, December 03, 2002. Online at http://www.sec.gov/news/press/2002-173.htm

54. *United States of America v. Samuel Waksal,* Indictment, 02 Cr.

55. Farrell, Greg, "ImClone's Waksal given 7-year prison term," *USA Today*, June 10, 2003.

56. "Federal Judge Appoints WorldCom Monitor," Reuters, July 3, 2002.

57. "Six months after Sept. 11, hijackers' visa approval letters received," CNN.com, March 13, 2002.

58. *Securities and Exchange Commission v. Arthur A. Goodwin, William J. Burke and Christopher P. Whalen,* (United States District Court for the District of Massachusetts) Civil Action No. 02 CV 11913 JLT.

59. Destruction Of Enron-Related Documents by Andersen Personnel, Hearing Before the Subcommittee On Oversight And Investigations Of The Committee On Energy And Commerce, House Of Representatives, One Hundred Seventh Congress, Second Session, January 24, 2002, Serial No. 107-80.

60. "Federal Prosecution of Corporations," Department of Justice Memorandum to Component Heads and United States Attorneys, June 16, 1999.

61. United States Sentencing Commission News Release, "Sentencing Commission Convenes Organizational Guidelines Ad Hoc Advisory Group," Thursday, February 21, 2002.

62. "Federal Prosecution of Corporations," Department of Justice Memorandum to Component Heads and United States Attorneys, June 16, 1999.

63. *In re Caremark International Inc. Derivative Litigation,* Del. Chancery C.A. 13670, 698 A.2d 959, 970 (September 25, 1996).

64. United States Sentencing Commission News Release, "Sentencing Commission Convenes Organizational Guidelines Ad Hoc Advisory Group," Thursday, February 21, 2002.

65. At the time this book was written (Fall 2003), the U.S. Sentencing Commission was reviewing Chapter 8 of the Guidelines, and specifically the compliance guidance provided there, to determine if should be updated or expanded to address the widespread influence that it has had, and to respond to Sarbanes-Oxley.

Chapter 6

66. Worthen, Ben, "Your Risks and Responsibilities: You may think the Sarbanes-Oxley legislation has nothing to do with you. You'd be wrong," *CIO Magazine*, May 15, 2003.

67. Pub. L. 107-204, 116 Stat. 745 (2002).

68. "Senior Executives Less Favorable On Sarbanes-Oxley, PricewaterhouseCoopers Finds," PricewaterhouseCoopers Management Barometer, July 23, 2003.

69. Nyberg, Alix, "Sticker Shock," *CFO Magazine*, September 8, 2003.

70. "Poultry firm settles first Sarbanes-Oxley charge," Reuters, August 18, 2003.

71. "Former Ernst & Young Audit Partner Arrested for Obstruction Charges and Criminal Violations of Sarbanes-Oxley Act," U.S. Department of Justice Press Release, September 25, 2003.

72. "President's Corporate Fraud Task Force Compiles Strong Record," White House Office of the Press Secretary Fact Sheet, July 22, 2003. Online at http://www.whitehouse.gov/news/releases/2003/07/20030722.html

73. Including, for example, Regulation S-K, S-B, S-X, and Exchange Act Rules 13a-14, 13a-15, 15d-14, and 15d-15.

74. "President Bush Signs Corporate Corruption Bill," White House Office of the Press Secretary, July 30, 2002. Online at http://www.whitehouse.gov/news/releases/2002/07/20020730.html

75. The term "public company" is used broadly here to include a range of entities that come under the SEC's jurisdiction. There may be cases where private companies are affected, such as when they have a public bond offering, for example.

76. "President's Corporate Fraud Task Force Compiles Strong Record," White House Office of the Press Secretary Fact Sheet, July 22, 2003. Online at http://www.whitehouse.gov/news/releases/2003/07/20030722.html

77. Pub. L. 107-204, 116 Stat. 745 (2002), SEC. 802.

78. Ibid., SEC. 404.

79. Ibid., SEC. 302.

80. Ibid., SEC. 906.

81. SEC Release No. 33-8328, "Management's Reports on Internal Control Over Financial Reporting and Certification of Disclosure in Exchange Act Periodic Reports," June 5, 2003.

Chapter 7

82. *In re Prudential Ins. Co. of America Sales Practices Litigation,* 169 F.R.D. 598 (D.N.J. 1997).

83. Ibid.

84. *Kentucky Cent. Life Ins. Co. v. Jones,* 1993 U.S. App. LEXIS 21976.

85. "SEC, NYSE, NASD Fine Five Firms Total of $8.25 Million for Failure To Preserve E-Mail Communications," SEC press release, December 03, 2002.

86. *Faragher v. City of Boca Raton,* 524, U.S. 775 (1998).

Chapter 8

87. *Palmer v. Lenfest Group,* 2000 Del. Super. LEXIS 81.

88. "Guidance for Industry, Part 11, Electronic Records; Electronic Signatures—Scope and Application," FDA, February 2003.

89. See, for example, "Guidance for Industry, Part 11, Electronic Records; Electronic Signatures—Scope and Application," FDA, February 2003.

90. "Eli Lilly Settles FTC Charges Concerning Security Breach," FTC Press Release, January 18, 2002.

Chapter 9

91. *Email Policies and Practices: An Industry Study Conducted by AIIM International and Kahn Consulting, Inc.,* 2003. AIIM International and Kahn Consulting jointly conducted the Study in Q3 2003. Over 1,000 respondents representing small and large organizations in the public sector and all major industries participated in the survey.

92. *Cabnetware, Inc. v. Sullivan,* 1991 U.S. Dist. LEXIS 20329.

93. *Bills v. Kennecott Corp.,* 108 F.R.D. 459, 462 (D. Utah 1985).

94. FED. RUL. CIV. PROC. 26(a)(1)(B).

95. Ibid. 34(a).

96. *FTC v. Toysmart.com, LLC, and Toysmart.com, Inc.* Online at http://www.ftc.gov/opa/2000/07/toysmart.htm

97. *Garrity v. John Hancock Mut. Life Ins. Co.,* 146 Lab. Cas. (CCH).

98. Robertson, Rob, "NASD ruling 'unprecedented' in Duncan-Williams victory," *Memphis Business Journal*, August 18, 2003.

99. "Summary of 'Lessons Learned' from Events of September 11 and Implications for Business Continuity," Securities and Exchange Commission, February 13, 2002.

100. Verton, Dan, "Power industry unveils $100B upgrade plan," *Computerworld*, August 25, 2003.

101. "Records Management Guidance For PKI-Unique Administrative Records," National Archives and Records Administration, March 14, 2003.

102. "Business Benefits of Telecommuting," Economist Intelligence Unit report, eMarketer, July 17, 2003.

103. "Notebooks Claim Over 50% of Retail PC Sales," NPD Group report, eMarketer, July 9, 2003.

104. "Hotspots: Hot Wireless Initiative," Yankee Group and Gartner Dataquest reports, eMarketer, July 8, 2003.

105. "Business Benefits of Telecommuting," Economist Intelligence Unit report, eMarketer, July 17, 2003.

106. "Notebooks Claim Over 50% of Retail PC Sales," NPD Group report, eMarketer, July 9, 2003.

107. "Queens Man Pleads Guilty to Federal Charges of Computer Damage, Access Device Fraud and Software Piracy," U.S. Department of Justice Press Release, July 11, 2003.

108. Guth, Robert A., and Daniel Machalaba, "Computer Viruses Disrupt Railroad and Air Traffic," *The Wall Street Journal*, August 21, 2003.

109. Verton, Dan, "Blaster Worm Linked to Severity of Blackout," *Computerworld*, September 1, 2003.

110. CERT website—http://www.cert.org/stats/

Chapter 10

111. Sine Qua Non: an absolute prerequisite.

112. *United States ex rel. Koch v. Koch Indus.,* 1999 U.S. Dist. LEXIS 16621 (U.S. Dist., 1999).

113. "Johnson & Johnson Faces FDA Probe," *Washington Post*, July 19, 2002.

114. "Overtime and the American Worker," a study by Cornell University Institute for Workplace Studies, 1999.

115. *SEC v. Lawrence O'Shaughnessy, Gary H. Klein, Gary K. Levi and Mark Tucker,* Civil Action No. 03 CV 3022 (RMB), April 30, 2003.

116. *In re Prudential Ins. Co. of America Sales Practices Litigation,* 169 F.R.D. 598 (D.N.J. 1997).

117. *Mobil Oil Corporation v. Grinnell Corporation and Diversified Information Technologies Inc.,* No. 190-C-1999; 2953-C-1999.

118. *Danis v. USN Communications, Inc.,* 2000 WL 1694325, N.D.Ill., 2000.

Chapter 11

119. *In Re Three Grand Jury Subpoenas Duces Tecum,* 191 F.3d 173 (2 Cir., 1999).

120. *Gloves, Inc. v. Berger,* 198 F.R.D. 6.

Chapter 12

121. Johnson, Maryfran, "Sarbanes Action Plan," *Computerworld,* June 2, 2003.

122. McMillan, Robert, "Survey: U.S. business, IT executives at odds on disaster recovery," IDG News Service, July 14, 2003.

123. The Radicati Group and Merrill Lynch as quoted by Helene Zampetakis, "Talk is cheap, email is not," *The Age,* July 8, 2003.

124. *Applied Telematics v. Sprint,* 1996 U.S. Dist. LEXIS 14053 (D. Pa.).

125. According to regulations such as: Securities and Exchange Commission (SEC) Rule 17a-4, National Association of Securities Dealers (NASD) Conduct Rules 3010 and 3110, and New York Stock Exchange (NYSE) Rule 440.

126. Connor, Deni, "Government regs taxing on storage resources," *Network World,* July 15, 2003.

127. This lists of e-discovery costs comes from "Electronic Discovery: From Novelty to Target," Randolph Kahn, ESQ., and Barclay T. Blair, and published by Legato Systems. Readers interested in e-discovery issues should consult this paper, available at the Kahn Consulting website at http://www.kahnconsultinginc.com/library

128. *In re Prudential Ins. Co. of America Sales Practices Litigation,* 169 F.R.D. 598 (D.N.J. 1997).

129. *Murphy Oil USA, Inc. v. Fluor Daniel, Inc.,* 2002 U.S. Dist. LEXIS 3196 (U.S. Dist., 2002).

130. *Mobil Oil Corporation v. Grinnell Corporation and Diversified Information Technologies Inc.,* No. 190-C-1999; 2953-C-1999.

131. *Maine Public Utilities Commission Order,* 2003 Me. PUC LEXIS 181, April 30, 2003.

Chapter 13

132. *People v. Bovio,* 118 Ill. App. 3d 836 (Ill. App., 1983).

133. *Danis v. USN Communications, Inc.,* 2000 WL 1694325, N.D.Ill., 2000.

134. Saffady, William, and ARMA International, "Records and Information Management, A Benchmarking Study of Large U.S. Industrial Companies," 2002.

135. *United States v. Van Riper,* 154 F.2d 492; 1946 U.S. App. LEXIS 2070.

Chapter 15

136. Zetter, Kim, "BlackBerry Reveals Bank's Secrets," Wired News, August 25, 2003. Online at http://www.wired.com/news/business/0,1367,60052-3,00.html

137. *Garrity v. John Hancock Mut. Life Ins. Co.,* 146 Lab. Cas. (CCH) P59, 541.

138. Ibid.

139. *Testa v. Wal-Mart Stores,* 144 F.3d 173.

140. *Email Policies and Practices: An Industry Study Conducted by AIIM International and Kahn Consulting, Inc.,* 2003.

Chapter 16

141. *Smith v. Texaco,* 951 F. Supp. 109 (U.S. Dist., 1997).

142. "Federal Judge Appoints WorldCom Monitor," Reuters, July 3, 2002.

143. *State ex rel. Dispatch Printing Co. v. City of Columbus,* 90 Ohio St. 3d 39 (Ohio, 2000).

144. "Contract to shred documents doesn't trump records law," The News Media & The Law, Fall 2000 (Vol. 24, No. 4), Page 35.

145. Rosencrance, Linda, "InstallShield sues competitor Wise Solutions for electronic espionage," *Computerworld,* July 18, 2003.

146. CERT® Advisory CA-1993-10 Anonymous FTP Activity.

147. IRS Revenue Procedure 97-22 Section 4.

148. Ibid., Section 5.

149. Ibid., Section 7.

150. These seven principles are: Notice, Choice, Onward Transfer, Security, Data Integrity, Access, and Enforcement.

151. "Safe Harbor Privacy Principles," U.S. Department of Commerce, July 21, 2000.

152. "Safe Harbor FAQ 7—Verification," U.S. Department of Commerce. Online at http://www.export.gov/safeharbor/Faq7verifFINAL.htm

153. *Garrity v. John Hancock Mut. Life Ins. Co.,* 146 Lab. Cas. (CCH).

154. Ibid.

155. Weiss, Todd R., "Software piracy shows decline since '94," *Computerworld,* June 3, 2003.

Key #6

156. "Federal Prosecution of Business Organizations," Department of Justice Memorandum to Heads of Department Components and United States Attorneys, January 2003.

Chapter 17

157. *Garrity v. John Hancock Mut. Life Ins. Co.,* 146 Lab. Cas. (CCH).

158. *Autoliv Asp v. Dep't of Workforce Servs.,* 2001 UT App 198.

159. Ibid.

160. *Flynn v. Raytheon Co.,* 868 F. Supp. 383.

Chapter 19

161. *Email Policies and Practices: An Industry Study Conducted by AIIM International and Kahn Consulting, Inc.,* 2003.

162. *Autoliv Asp v. Dep't of Workforce Servs.,* 2001 UT App 198.

163. "Is IM a Sieve for Corporate Secrets?" IDC, as reported by PCWorld.com, July 19, 2002.

164. "National Archives and Records Administration's Acquisition of Major System Faces Risks," GAO Highlights, August 2003.

165. *Carr v. El Dorado Chem. Co.,* 1997 U.S. Dist. LEXIS 5752.

166. Ibid.

167. Ibid.

Index

FRE *See* Federal Rules of Evidence

FTC *See* Federal Trade Commission

FTP *See* file transfer protocol

Gamber-Johnson v. Trans Data Net Corp. 40

GAO *See* General Accounting Office

gap analysis 250, 251

Garrity v. John Hancock Mut. Life Ins. Co. 112, 189, 216, 224

General Accounting Office 246

General Motors *See Moore v. ...*

Gloves, Inc. v. Berger 145

hardware (computer) 14, 23, 38, 39, 40, 98, 108, 118, 150, 199
See also information technology; mobile devices

Health Insurance Portability and Accountability Act 87, 166, 171, 212

hearsay rule 27-28

HHS *See* Department of Health and Human Services

HIPAA *See* Health Insurance Portability and Accountability Act

ILM *See* lifecycle management

imaging 48, 73, 91, 111, 204-205

IMC *See* information management compliance

indexing 38, 48, 73, 91, 107

information assets 33-34, 110-111, 117, 134, 259

information growth 9, 23, 148, 149, 242

information lifecycle management
See lifecycle management

information management 4, 11, 13-14, 16, 44-46, 72-72

information management compliance

- continuous improvement 241-257

- criteria 43-44, 46-47

- enforcement 221-238

- failures 15, 50-55, 58-60, 82-84, 101, 152-161

- monitoring 203-218

- organization 175-183

- programs 3, 44-46, 65

- responsibility for 5, 127-139, 141-145, 165-173, 175-183

- seven keys to 3-4, 57-63

information privacy *See* privacy

information security *See* security

information technology 9, 16, 40-41, 48, 59-60, 91, 95-97, 103-105, 117-123, 131-132, 231-238
See also name of specific technologies

instant messaging 9, 18, 23, 28, 60, 80, 86-87, 98, 103, 104, 106, 148, 200, 218, 235-236, 242, 245
See also digital information

Institute of Certified Records Managers 167

Industry Resources

Kahn Consulting, Inc.

157 Leonard Wood North
Highland Park, IL 60035
847-266-0722
www.KahnConsultingInc.com

Kahn Consulting, Inc. ("KCI"), is a consulting firm specializing in the legal, compliance, and policy issues of information technology, information management, and records management. Through a range of services including information management program development, risk management audits, policy development and evaluation, product assessments, legal and compliance research, and education and training, KCI helps its clients address today's critical issues in an ever-changing regulatory and technological environment. Based in Chicago, KCI provides its services to Fortune 500 companies and state and federal governmental agencies in North America and around the world.

AIIM

1100 Wayne Avenue, Suite 1100
Silver Spring, MD 20910 USA
800-477-2446 / 301-587-8202
aiim@aiim.org
www.aiim.org

AIIM Europe
The IT Centre, 8 Canalside,
Lowesmoor Wharf, Worcester
WR1 2RR, UK
+44 (0) 1905 727600
info@aiim.org.uk
www.aiim.org.uk

For over 60 years, AIIM has been the leading international organization focused on helping users understand the challenges associated with managing documents, content, and business processes. AIIM's core values reflect this long-term perspective:

- International – Members in over 75 countries

- Independent – Unbiased and vendor neutral

- Implementation Focused – Processes, not just technology

- Industry Intermediary – Users, suppliers, consultants, analysts, and the channel

AIIM defines Enterprise Content Management (ECM) as the technologies used to capture, manage, store, preserve, and deliver content and documents related to organizational processes. The ECM industry provides information management solutions to help users:

- guarantee business CONTINUITY, 24x7x365

- enable employee, partner, and customer COLLABORATION

- ensure legal and regulatory COMPLIANCE

- reduce COSTS through process streamlining and standardization

Key AIIM Products and Services

For more detail, see the AIIM website at *www.aiim.org*.

Market Education – AIIM provides events and information services that help users specify, select and deploy ECM solutions to solve organizational problems.

- *AIIM E-DOC Magazine* – Published six times per year, the industry's leading magazine in North America.

- *mID* (Managing Information and Documents) – Published six times per year in partnership with Infoconomy, the leading publication for the industry in the UK.

- *Content Management Seminar Series* – General and vertically focused educational seminars held in 20 cities per year throughout the U.S. and Canada.

- *IM Expo* – The major educational event for the ECM industry, held in five or six locations each year across the United Kingdom.

- *InfoIreland* – A two-day educational event held annually in Ireland.

Professional Development – AIIM provides an educational roadmap for the industry.

- *IM University* – A multifaceted education program (Web-based education, single-day events, and multi-day residential programs) offered in Europe.

- *Fundamentals of ECM Certificate Program* – A Web-based professional certificate program designed to help users become familiar with the core concepts and technologies related to Information Management Compliance.

- *AIIM Webinars* – Typically attracting over 500 attendees per session, AIIM webinars provide education on the key issues and trends affecting the industry.

Peer Networking – Through chapters, networking groups, programs, partnerships, and the Web, AIIM creates opportunities that allow, users, suppliers, consultants, and the channel to engage and connect with one another.

- *AIIM Show and Conference* – Produced by Advanstar Communications in cooperation with AIIM, this is the premier networking and education event for the industry.

- *AIIM Chapters* – A network of 39 chapters in North America providing educational and networking opportunities at the local level for AIIM members.

- *AIIM Partners* – A global network of organizations similar to AIIM committed to helping grow the industry.

- *AIIM ChannelConnection* – A special series of programs and services specifically designed for document and content management VARs, System Integrators, and Service Companies.

Industry Advocacy – AIIM acts as the voice of the ECM industry in key standards organizations, with the media and with government decision-makers.

- *Industry Watch* – AIIM user-focused industry research and analysis.

- *AIIM Standards* – AIIM is an ANSI (American National Standards Institute) accredited standards development organization. AIIM also holds the Secretariat for the ISO (International Organization for Standardization) committee focused on Information Management Compliance issues, TC171.

Documentum, Inc.

a division of EMC

6801 Koll Center Parkway
Pleasanton, CA 94566-7047
925-600-6800
Fax: 925-600-6850
www.documentum.com

Documentum – Putting Content in Motion

Documentum provides enterprise content management (ECM) solutions that enable companies to unite teams, content, and associated business processes. Documentum's integrated set of content, compliance, and collaboration solutions support the way people work, from initial discussion and planning through design, production, marketing, sales, service, and corporate administration. With a single platform, Documentum enables people to collaboratively create, manage, deliver, and archive information that drives business operations—from documents, records, and discussions to email, Web pages, and rich media. The Documentum platform makes it possible for companies to distribute all of this content in multiple languages, across internal and external systems, applications, and user communities.

Documentum's customers, which include the world's most successful organizations, harness corporate knowledge, accelerate time to market, increase customer satisfaction, enhance supply chain efficiencies, and reduce operating costs—improving their overall competitive advantage.

Founded in 1990, Documentum was the first to market with an enterprise-scale document management solution built from standard relational database technologies in combination with object-oriented methodologies. Soon, pharmaceutical firms; oil and gas corporations; federal, state and local government agencies; and other large enterprises came to rely on Documentum to systematically control the production and distribution of mission-critical documents. As the Internet evolved, Documentum set the pace in helping companies leverage the Web to conduct business, by extending its platform to enable Web content management.

Using the Documentum platform, companies streamlined management of Web sites and extended the use and value of documents and other content, sharing it with other audiences on the Web. Documentum then expanded into digital asset management, records management, compliance, and collaboration solutions. As a result, Documentum is the first and only vendor to offer a complete ECM solution in one integrated platform. This includes best-ofbreed document management, records management, Web content management, digital asset management, collaboration, and compliance technologies, as well as business process automation.

Documentum Products

From online commerce and 24x7 customer service to online procurement and collaborative project management, Documentum confidently controls and delivers the knowledge critical for every e-business process.

No other enterprise solution can equal Documentum with its ability to manage Web content, power portals, enable collaborative commerce, and solve regulatory and compliance challenges. Documentum provides a mix of products, world-class consulting, customer education, and 24x7x365 support to address the following e-business initiatives and requirements:

- Increasing the efficiency of business operations by effectively managing business-critical content

- Enabling applications, including ERP, CRM, Enterprise Information Portal, and groupware systems with enterprise content and collaboration

- Capturing knowledge and experience with Web-based collaboration tools

- Accelerating time to Web with accurate, reliable information

- Enabling rich media asset management integrated with enterprise content

- Providing integrated records management to create, safeguard, and access records according to legal, regulatory, or administrative rules

- Managing XML components to fuel content reuse and dynamic publishing

- Automating the production, review, approval, and publishing of all marketing assets

- Meeting regulatory compliance with trusted content

- Supporting the development of content-rich applications built on a solid, future-proof platform

For more information, call us at 800-607-9546 or visit us online at *www.documentum.com.*

Eastman Kodak Company

343 State Street
Rochester, NY 14650-1181
800-944-6171
bistech@cyber.kodak.com
www.kodak.com/go/us-di

Infoimaging@Kodak

Kodak's imaging technologies have enabled the management and comprehension of information for over 75 years. Kodak empowers information processes with imaging, because we understand that the combination of both is the best approach for efficient information exchange. It's called infoimaging and it's the lifeblood of commercial and government organizations throughout the world. Analyzing information provides the insights necessary to manage risk, minimize operations costs, and optimize interactions with partners, supply chains, and customers.

The spirit of innovation and serving customer needs are core principles that are delivered in the form of infoimaging products and services. Infoimaging is a $385 billion industry created by the convergence of information technology and imaging science. And, Kodak is at the heart of it. The power of pictures coupled with information creates the perfect harmony between people and technology.

Data can take you only so far. To complete the big picture, you require access to formatted documents and a variety of pictorial information. That's where Kodak's infoimaging solutions come in. We enable images as a part of workflows and information repositories in order to improve your abilities to:

- Automate process workflows

- Access information quickly

- Trust the integrity of information

- Detect changes readily

- Communicate efficiently

Who better than Kodak for Infoimaging?

At Kodak, we have the resources and tools to help you envision the possibilities—and potential—offered through the marriage of image science and information technology. Our imaging experience and portfolios of patents and products are unsurpassed. If you use images, chances are we can improve your processes with one or more of our technologies. If you market image-enabled products or services, we may be able to shorten your time to market and improve your competitive position with hardware, enabling software, and processing technologies. We're ready to partner with customers and developers to innovate the next generation of connecting end-users with images.

Drive more value from your information with imaging science from Kodak.

We can help you integrate imaging into your processes in order to improve end-user comprehension. Our solutions can mitigate risk and maintain the survivability of information. Imaging can be used to reduce storage and data migration requirements and resolve inter-platform issues.

We have the people, processes, and technology to significantly amplify how you use your information. To get started putting imaging to work for you, just call us at 800-243-8811 and request a copy of A-5727 *Empower Your Enterprise*.

FileNet Corporation

 **3565 Harbor Blvd**
Costa Mesa, CA 92626-1420
800-FileNet (345-3638) / 714-327-3400
International: 714-327-4800
www.filenet.com/compliance

In today's marketplace, ensuring regulatory compliance and good corporate governance has become a critical—and increasingly costly—business challenge. It is made more complex by the changeable nature of compliance itself and the fact that compliance today by no means ensures compliance tomorrow.

As a result, many companies are now actively seeking compliance solutions that are comprised of proven, scalable technologies that can be rapidly deployed and modified to address both current and future regulatory requirements. These solutions require enterprise-class content and process management capabilities to enable a much more comprehensive and value-driven approach to ensuring compliance.

FileNet Corporation helps organizations make better, faster decisions by managing the content and processes that drive their business. FileNet's Enterprise Content Management (ECM) solutions allow customers to build and sustain competitive advantage by managing content throughout their organizations, automating and streamlining their business processes, and providing the full spectrum of connectivity needed to enable critical and everyday decision-making.

FileNet ECM offers organizations a compliance framework that delivers control over critical business information through a combination of content, process, and connectivity. While Content Management provides both enhanced visibility and control over critical information, Business Process Management drives the very processes that comprise an organization's compliance efforts. When employed in conjunction with FileNet's comprehensive records management and forms management capabilities, FileNet ECM provides an effective and scalable platform for compliance.

FileNet's Compliance Framework forms an essential foundation for addressing many of today's compliance requirements. FileNet's Compliance Framework is not simply a point solution for Sarbanes-Oxley; rather, it is a framework that can be employed to address Sarbanes-Oxley, HIPAA, the U.S.

Patriot Act, FDA, EPA, SEC 17a-4 and many other compliance issues facing today's businesses. Because compliance management is a moving target, FileNet's Compliance Framework is also extremely flexible and adaptable to future regulatory requirements, enabling organizations to rapidly deploy new or modify existing compliance processes and programs.

In short, FileNet's Compliance Framework helps corporations to address today's regulatory requirements while effectively positioning them to rapidly respond to future legislation and the changing face of compliance. FileNet's Compliance Framework:

- Reduces the cost of compliance through process acceleration, automation, and instantaneous access to vital corporate content

- Enhances corporate transparency, providing top-down visibility into critical compliance processes, information, and controls

- Enables enterprise-wide contribution to compliance efforts, proactively managing the build, approval, and reporting of required information

- Reduces the risk of fines, penalties, and litigation resulting from non-compliance

- Enables organizations to be more responsive by immediately identifying and reacting to material events.

- Enhances business continuity and fail-over capabilities

- Ensures that vital corporate records are effectively declared, securely maintained, and properly destroyed at the end of their lifecycle

Since the Company's founding in 1982, more than 4,000 organizations, including 81 of the *Fortune 100*, have taken advantage of FileNet solutions for help in managing their mission-critical content and processes.

Headquartered in Costa Mesa, Calif., FileNet markets its innovative ECM solutions in more than 90 countries through its own global sales, professional services, and support organizations, as well as via its ValueNet® Partner network of resellers, system integrators, and application developers.

Hitachi Data Systems Corporation

750 Central Expressway
Santa Clara, CA 95050-2627
408-970-1000
Fax: 408-727-8036
info@hds.com
www.hds.com

Hitachi Data System provides market-driven solutions, based on industry-leading storage systems and management software, that solve business problems through strategic consulting, design, integration, and robust deployment capability. Our initial data lifecycle management focus is on message content—an area of extreme importance to financial services, life sciences, healthcare, government, and retail clients.

"Hitachi Data Systems has taken a strategic look at integrating products and services to provide email management today, and broader unstructured content capabilities in the future," said Ken Beaudry, Senior Vice President and General Manager, Global Solution Services, Hitachi Data Systems. "We aren't asking customers to learn and manage a second, non-standard storage infrastructure. What we've come up with is unlike anything being described by others in the market—and the solutions GSS has designed can be extended to provide archive and retention for a wide range of content types and for specific vertical industries."

Delivered by the company's Global Solution Services (GSS) division, HDS helps address the growing need to store and manage email and other unstructured content with the following offerings:

Message Archive for Compliance solution enables companies to retain an unalterable archive of email and instant messages for the fixed period of time mandated by key regulatory requirements. This solution is fully indexed and searchable, allowing companies to more efficiently respond to audits, discovery requests, or other situations where prompt delivery of unaltered email is critical.

Message Archive for Email removes difficult-to-administer email inbox size limits. Administrators and end users can establish archival rules that migrate messages from primary to secondary storage yet preserve the client interface—making archived email readily accessible, searchable, and retrievable.

Archival Policy Design Service helps customers institute policies that remove the challenge of administering burgeoning email infrastructures and satisfy email-specific regulations.

Hitachi Data Systems conducts business through direct and indirect channels in the public, government and private sectors in over 170 countries. Its customers include more than 50% of Fortune 100 companies. For more information, please visit our website at *www.hds.com*.

Hyland Software, Inc.

28500 Clemens Road
Westlake, OH 44145
440-788-5000
Fax: 440-788-5100
hyland@onbase.com
www.onbase.com

Hyland Software, established in 1991, is the leading provider of rapidly deployable enterprise content management solutions. The company's flagship product is OnBase, enterprise-class software that combines integrated document management, business process management, and records management in a single Web-enabled application. OnBase solutions allow organizations to increase productivity and reduce costs while satisfying compliance requirements.

With the ability to handle thousands of users and terabytes of data, OnBase electronically captures, stores, and manages literally every document generated or received by your company—including paper, reports, application files, emails, audio, video, and Web content. It can manage everything you need to do with those documents—create, store, retrieve, revise, annotate, distribute, post to a website, or purge. OnBase manages the flow of those documents and streamlines or automates the processes in which they are involved. In addition, OnBase integrates seamlessly with your ERP, CRM, and other core business applications to create a single point of online access to all relevant information and process workflow.

Solutions:

Hyland Software, Inc. has affiliations with a global network of value-added resellers, integrators, and private-label partnerships. The unique architecture of the software and diversity of expertise among the company's channel partners have allowed OnBase to be implemented in a remarkably wide range of commercial and public sector organizations.

Business Solutions	Industry Solutions
■ Accounts payable	■ Education
■ Accounts receivable	■ Financial services
■ Customer service	■ Government
■ Credentialing	• Federal
■ Disaster recovery	• State, county, and local
■ E-commerce	■ Healthcare
■ Expense reporting	■ Housing authorities
■ ISO 9001 support	■ Insurance
■ Compliance support/reporting	■ Manufacturing/transportation
■ Electronic statement/bill presentment	■ Utilities
■ Human resources	

Interwoven, Inc.

★ INTERWOVEN

803 11th Avenue
Sunnyvale, CA 94089
888-468-3796 / 408-774-2000
compliance@interwoven.com
www.interwoven.com

Collaborative Document Management, Email Management, Business Process Automation, and Records Management

Interwoven, Inc. is the world's next-generation enterprise content management (ECM) company. The Interwoven ECM platform provides complete content life-cycle management, including Collaborative Document Management, Email Management, Content Management, Business Process Automation, and Records Management, all through a secure, configurable, and interactive Portal Interface. The company's 2,700 customers include 32 of the Global 50 including Air France, Cisco Systems, General Electric, General Motors and Yamaha.

Enhanced with Sarbanes-Oxley Act and Corporate Governance templates and workflows and featuring tight integration with Microsoft Office, Outlook, and Lotus Notes, the Interwoven WorkSite suite of applications provides companies with a comprehensive, yet quick-to-deploy, platform for financial compliance.

Interwoven WorkSite can be used to address an array of compliance initiatives including:

- **Collaborative Document Authoring:** Sophisticated document management functionality enables the development and dissemination of policies and procedures for business processes, self-assessment surveys, control definition, remediation plans, and ongoing monitoring. Integration with leading COSO frameworks ensures that process and content are tightly linked.

- **Board of Directors Communication:** A dedicated, centrally accessible WorkSpace is used to share and capture meeting logistics, minutes, and correspondence for secure and effective corporate governance. Full audit trails allow easy determination of when content was accessed or modified and by whom.

- **Internal and External Audit:** WorkSpaces make it easy to securely collaborate and communicate compliance-specific issues with regulators, and internal and external auditors. Business process automation functions automate and ensure compliance with key processes.

- **Preparation and Approval of Financial Statements:** Collaborative document management facilitates the collection of data and creation and approval of financial statements with complete version control and audit trails.

IXOS SOFTWARE AG

Technopark 1
Bretonischer Ring 12
D-85630 Grasbrunn
Germany
+49 (0) 89 4629 0
Fax: +49 (0) 89 4629 1199
office@ixos.de
www.ixos.com

IXOS SOFTWARE, INC.
901 Marineer's Island Boulevard
Suite 725
San Mateo, CA 94404
650-294-5500/650-294-5800
Fax: 650-294-5836
info@ixos.com
www.ixos.com

IXOS is a leading provider of Enterprise Content Management (ECM) solutions. The IXOS offering ranges from solutions for the efficient management and display of Web information, to optimization of business processes, all the way to the secure, long-term archiving of all business documents in a dependable document repository.

IXOS builds and delivers software solutions to help companies address stringent requirements for operational efficiency, IT consolidation, risk reduction, and knowledge sharing. Business information and corporate knowledge, also described as content, is a company's life-blood, its raison d'être. IXOS's Enterprise Content Management (ECM) solutions enable our customers to create, deliver, and manage any content throughout and outside their enterprise—business application data, documents, email, Web pages, and rich media—using a common content repository and architecture. IXOS products integrate hand-in-glove with a company's existing software environment, be it SAP, Siebel, Microsoft, Lotus Notes, a portal, or a line-of-business applications.

IXOS solutions facilitate the capitalization and sharing of knowledge. They enhance and speed up internal and external business processes. They also help optimize the IT infrastructure. This results in improved services to the company's own employees, to its business partners, and to its end customers.

With offices in 17 countries and a worldwide network of certified Distributors and Resellers, IXOS maintains a global team of highly qualified consultants, who support its comprehensive range of Enterprise Content Management solutions. Our Support Centers cover three continents and work around the clock, all year long, to serve the needs of our local and global customers. IXOS partnerships with leading international hardware and software vendors, as well as system integrators, guarantee the deployment of innovative technology and comprehensive industry expertise.

For these reasons, thousands of enterprises worldwide, including most of the Fortune 500 companies, have chosen IXOS as a key strategic partner. This represents more than 1.75 million users working in a variety of industries: banks and insurance companies, the public sector and utilities, automobile manufacturers, pharmaceutical and chemical companies, as well as retailers. Most of the Global 500 is represented, as are such industrial giants as General Motors, Microsoft, Lufthansa Cargo, Aventis, Barclays Bank, and Samsung.

Its financial stability makes IXOS a stable, long-term partner. Major corporations from a wide variety of industries have already installed over 3,000 IXOS installations worldwide—enabling them to reduce their costs and simultaneously enhance their productivity and competitiveness. More than 2 million users around the world already work with ECM solutions from IXOS.

Founded in 1988, IXOS is currently listed on the NASDAQ and the Frankfurt Stock Exchange in Germany. Shares of IXOS SOFTWARE AG are traded under the symbol "XOS" in the Prime Standard segment of the Frankfurt Stock Exchange (ISIN: DE0005061501). In the U.S., American Depository Shares (ADS) are traded on NADSAQ under the symbol "XOSY." IXOS stock is part of the TechDAX30 index. For more information, please see *www.ixos.com*.

LEGATO Software

 A division of EMC
2350 West El Camino Real
Mountain View, CA 94040
888-853-4286
Fax: 650-210-7032
insidesales@legato.com
www.legato.com

LEGATO Software, a division of EMC Corporation, is a global provider of open, enterprise-class software solutions and services for Information Management—helping organizations to enable business continuity and compliance at the lowest total cost of ownership (TCO). LEGATO's information protection, automated availability, and messaging and content management solutions are delivered through a worldwide network of strategic partnerships and alliances, as well as a direct sales force.

LEGATO's approach to Information Management:

- Improves operational efficiency through centralized management, automated business processes, and better information sharing

- Reduces risk by eliminating data loss, improving corporate governance by enabling stronger control over information, and helping to ensure regulatory compliance

- Enables immediate access to critical information, whether for business or compliance requirements

- Enhances business continuity through high performance backup and recovery, automated replication and failover, and monitoring of critical applications

A leader in content and message management

LEGATO is a leader in providing solutions that support the compliance objectives of today's enterprises. LEGATO's **ApplicationXtender®** enables organizations to effectively collect, organize, retain, and deliver their critical documents and information assets—through a comprehensive, integrated suite of imaging, document management, computer report management (COLD), and workflow services. ApplicationXtender works hand-in-hand with business applications such as Geographic Information Systems (GIS), Customer Relationship Management (CRM), Enterprise Resource Planning (ERP), and Financials, allowing organizations to better control business processes, legal risks, and operating costs while enhancing information accessibility and decision-making. As a result, enterprises have greater control over their business records, which means they have better control of their business.

With ApplicationXtender, enterprises gain a competitive advantage through fast, cost-effective access to a central pool of mission-critical information. This powerful suite offers key benefits including:

- Reduced costs through seamless integration to existing business applications and minimizing physical storage
- Elimination of time-consuming manual searches and/or sifting through unrelated information
- Improved productivity by delivering the right information to the right person at the right time
- Enhanced collaboration between users and departments through automated workflow management

LEGATO's **EmailXtender**® addresses the critical need to manage email and instant messages through automated archiving, granular search and retrieval, retention management, and monitoring for electronic messaging, including Microsoft Exchange, Lotus Notes/Domino, Unix SendMail, Bloomberg Mail, and various instant messaging applications. EmailXtender is a comprehensive, policy-based suite that automatically collects, organizes, retains, and retrieves messages/attachments. By creating and managing a central repository of email and other messages, EmailXtender helps reduce the cost of email storage, boosts end-user and administrator productivity, and controls risk by supporting compliance with regulations and corporate governance policies.

EmailXtender delivers "must-have" email management features, including:

- Automatically copying every message and attachment to a central repository
- Generating a full-text index of all messages/attachments
- Enabling intelligent search/retrieval by administrators, supervisors, and users
- Reducing email server stress and bottlenecks by seamlessly extending email message stores into low-cost and high-capacity storage devices

EmailXtender helps reduce costs by freeing up saturated email services, reducing email server backup time, and providing administrators with diagnostic tools to analyze email traffic and storage requirements. More importantly, EmailXtender helps manage email as a record of business, in accordance with rules of evidence.

More than 31,000 organizations worldwide trust LEGATO's information management solutions. We are helping our customers achieve their business goals with an application-focused approach, easy to manage products that enable fast implementation for a quick ROI, and through industry-leading customer service—and all at a price point that makes LEGATO an unsurpassed value.

Stellent, Inc.

STELLENT™ 7777 Golden Triangle Drive
Eden Prairie, MN 55344
800-989-8774 / 952-903-2000
Fax: 952-829-5424
www.stellent.com

International Offices
Canada: 905-530-2079
France: +33 1 46 91 83 01
Germany: +49 89 57959 195
Italy: +39 381 694596
Japan: +81 3 5456 5507
Netherlands: +31 30 602 9500
U.K.: +44 1753 894 500

Stellent, Inc. (*www.stellent.com*) is a global provider of content management solutions. Stellent offers a flexible, robust, and scalable content management solution that allows employees, customers, and partners to collaborate, contribute, and access business content anywhere worldwide.

One architecture. One user interface.

Stellent is differentiated by its unique approach to managing content. The Stellent® Universal Content Management system provides a single architecture that offers Web content management, document management, collaboration, records management, and digital asset management functionalities. The system enables customers to rapidly deploy line-of-business Web sites, such as employee portals and partner extranets, as well as enterprise-wide solutions that standardize content management for use by multiple sites and applications throughout an organization. The Stellent Content Management system offers the widest array of content contribution and content delivery mechanisms on the market, enabling any user to contribute any kind of content into the system for conversion, management and delivery to any kind of Web site or application. It also integrates with existing security systems and provides business personalization, content integration, distribution, and categorization features.

Impressive Customer List

Headquartered in Eden Prairie, Minn., Stellent maintains offices throughout the United States, Europe, and Asia-Pacific and has more than 1,500 customers, including much of the Global 2000. Its customer roster includes Procter & Gamble, Merrill Lynch, Los Angeles County, British Red Cross, ING,

Target Corp., Janus, Emerson Process Management, and various BlueCross BlueShield organizations across 15 states in the U.S.

Industry Leader

Stellent has been ranked one of the top three content management vendors by industry analyst firms Gartner Dataquest, Giga Information Group, and Aberdeen Group. And, Stellent has been recognized by a number of leading publications and organizations for its product innovation, market leadership and successful customer implementations. Recent honors include: "EContent 100" from *EContent*, recognizing the top 100 Companies in Digital Content; 2003 RealWare Award for "Best Enterprise Content Management Application" from *Transform*; "Trend-Setting Product of 2003" and "100 Companies That Matter in Knowledge Management" from *KMWorld*; one of "The Hottest Companies of 2003" and a Technology Enabler Award from *Start*; Basex Excellence Award; Best Solutions Award from the Government Technology Conference; and 2003 Editors' Choice Gold Award from *WebSphere Advisor Magazine*.

Product Innovation

Stellent was an early adopter of the open, standards-based Java architecture, integrating the technology into its first content management product more than seven years ago. Stellent continues its ongoing commitment to developing next-generation technologies with its J2EE-compliant Enterprise JavaBean, Java Server Pages, Universal Content Management architecture, and more.

Superior Services

Stellent is known for its exceptional customer support, training, and consulting services. These teams excel in three key areas: deep technical expertise, customer satisfaction, and flexible offerings. Stellent services professionals provide superior customer service through quick response time, effective troubleshooting, and the delivery of comprehensive technical solutions.

ZANTAZ, Inc.

ZANTAZ®

5671 Gibraltar Drive
Pleasanton, CA 94588
800-636-0095
info@zantaz.com
www.zantaz.com

ZANTAZ® is the leading provider of compliance technology and electronic discovery services and solutions to clients in financial services, government, and other regulated industries. ZANTAZ solutions help clients efficiently comply with industry regulations, respond to urgent litigation and regulatory audits, and mitigate the risks associated with today's complex legal and regulatory environment. Through proven digital archiving, supervision, and electronic discovery systems, highly scalable technology and records management expertise, ZANTAZ delivers customer-driven solutions with a high-level of security and confidentiality. These solutions enable companies to manage business risk, reduce costs, and strengthen regulatory compliance and industry best practices.

Email and Instant Message Archiving and Retrieval:
The Market Leader

ZANTAZ was first to market with email and IM archiving solutions designed specifically to address securities industry book and record retention, access, and retrieval requirements—in particular, SEC Rules 17a-3 and 17a-4; NASD Rules 2210, 3010, and 3110; NYSE Rule 342; CFTC Rule 1.31; and NFA Rule 2-9. Unlike conventional storage devices or mailbox extension products that claim to support compliance, ZANTAZ solutions are proven through years of successful operation in the real world of regulatory compliance.

SEC regulations require data to be secure from tampering, yet easily accessible. ZANTAZ solutions meet the most stringent security standards, while its proprietary indexing technology allows for fast searching and instant retrieval by authorized users. And they offer unprecedented, unmatched scalability to suit even the largest enterprises and their ever-expanding needs.

The core component of the ZANTAZ solution is the centrally managed, ZANTAZ Digital Safe™ archive repository for all digital documents and electronic correspondence, purpose-built to meet stringent SEC requirements.

Monitoring and Supervision: Best in Class

ZANTAZ compliance solutions incorporate powerful, efficient tools to monitor electronic communications—including email, instant messages, and attachments. Using sophisticated, intelligent linguistic analysis, the system screens every inbound, outbound, and internal email for any suggestion of regulatory or policy violations. Suspect communications are flagged for supervisory review. The result is a seamlessly integrated solution for data capture, archiving, retrieval, monitoring, and supervision—one that ensures compliance with employee supervision regulations, notably SEC Rule 17a-4, NASD Rule 3010, and NYSE Rule 342.

Data Restoration: No Job Too Big

With electronic data growing in volume every day, and electronic evidence becoming more critical in regulatory investigations, litigation, and audits, firms need to prepare for the likelihood that they'll have to produce electronic documents currently stored on backup tapes. Moreover, the SEC requires securities firms to retain all email and instant messages in an easily accessible location for at least two years—longer in some cases—in non-tamperable media.

Many firms do not address their data restoration needs until they are compelled to do so by a regulatory request or subpoena. Searching for historical information on backup tapes can be a costly drain on IT resources and personnel—which is why leading financial firms call ZANTAZ when they have an urgent need to produce electronic documents. Using proprietary tools and processes, ZANTAZ converts the data from backup tapes to a secure digital repository, where it can be searched in a fraction of the time—and at a fraction of the cost—involved in searching backup tapes.

With its highly scalable technology, ZANTAZ is uniquely equipped to handle the largest, most complex data restoration assignments. Earlier this year, the company announced completion of a multi-million dollar, dedicated data restoration facility, which is currently processing thousands of tapes containing millions of messages every month.

Increasingly, companies are taking proactive measures to transfer legacy data from backup tapes to the ZANTAZ Digital Safe. In doing so, they are ensuring compliance with SEC records retention requirements, while being prepared to respond quickly in the event of an investigation or audit—before they have to.

While a number of vendors offer different pieces of the compliance puzzle, only ZANTAZ offers end-to-end capabilities encompassing archiving and retrieval, monitoring and supervision, and data restoration-the essentials of electronic communication compliance. And only ZANTAZ is 100% focused on regulatory compliance and legal needs. That is why 65% of Wall Street's top securities firms entrust their sensitive, business-critical data to ZANTAZ. According to a May 2003 report by storage industry analysts, the Radicati Group, ZANTAZ dominates the hosted email archiving market with a 71% share. ZANTAZ has captured and archived billions of emails and restored tens of thousands of backup tapes for litigation and regulatory compliance needs. Find out how ZANTAZ can help your firm. Visit *www.zantaz.com*

About the Authors

Sally Higginson Photography

Randolph A. Kahn, ESQ.

Randolph A. Kahn is an attorney and internationally recognized authority on the legal, risk management, compliance, and policy issues of business information, information technology, electronic evidence, and records management. As founder and principal of Kahn Consulting, Inc. (*www.KahnConsultingInc.com*), Mr. Kahn leads a team of consultants who advise corporations and governmental agencies on a wide range of issues related to business information, information technology and records management. He has played an important role in the development of industry standards related to e-records, electronic business risk management, information security, and information management. Each year, Mr. Kahn conducts dozens of seminars and training programs for corporate and government institutions. He is an instructor at George Washington University and a columnist for an information technology magazine. Mr. Kahn has authored numerous articles for legal, industry, and mainstream publications and is regularly interviewed by a wide variety of media outlets. Mr. Kahn is the co-author of *E-Mail Rules: A Business Guide to Managing Policies, Security, and Legal Issues for E-Mail and Digital Communication,* published in 2003.

Mr. Kahn may be contacted at *rkahn@KahnConsultingInc.com* or 847-266-0722.

Barclay T. Blair

Barclay T. Blair is an internationally acclaimed author, speaker, and consultant specializing in the business, policy, and management issues of information technology. As director of the Technology Practice at Kahn Consulting, Mr. Blair advises Fortune 500 companies, software and hardware vendors, and government agencies on a broad range of information management issues. Mr. Blair is an executive editor of the *American Bar Association's PKI Assessment Guidelines,* published in 2003 after more than five years of drafting. Mr. Blair participated in the development of an XML protocol for secure, digitally signed XML documents, and is the author of a draft ISO standard addressing long-term electronic records preservation. Mr. Blair has authored and edited dozens of publications, has spoken internationally on information management matters, and has lectured at George Washington University and the University of Victoria. Prior to *Information Nation*, Mr. Blair edited and contributed to several books, including: *E-mail Rules* (AMACOM Books: 2003); *Secure Electronic Commerce* (Prentice Hall: 2001); *Beginning XML* (Wrox: 2000); and *Professional XML* (Wrox: 2000).

Mr. Blair may be contacted at *bblair@KahnConsultingInc.com* or 250-480-1248.